AF413685

FEAST

FAITH

FLOURISH

____

holistic wellness in light of eternity

by *KATIE GEARNS* and *SAMANTHA WORTHING*
Photographs by ELISSA VOSS

SOPHIA INSTITUTE PRESS
Manchester, New Hampshire

Sophia Institute Press
Box 5284, Manchester, NH 03108
1-800-888-9344

www.SophiaInstitute.com

Sophia Institute Press® is a registered trademark of Sophia Institute.

Hardcover ISBN 979-8-88911-524-3
ebook ISBN 979-8-88911-525-0
Library of Congress Control Number: 2025935011

First printing

To Kevin, thank you for being both my and Ember's biggest supporter. Your love and sacrifice helped make this all happen. And to André, Sophie, Margot, and baby boy — you are forever my inspiration. — KG

To Joseph, thank you for providing the strength and care to help me flourish. To my loves Maximilian, Norah, and Louisa, I am convicted because of you. And to Christine in your eternal home, who set me on this journey in the beginning, thank you from the bottom of my heart. — SW

To Mom, Dad, Mama, the Ember ladies, and every dear soul — family, friend, stranger — who has supported me on my journey to eternity, especially when I have been in the trenches of long suffering. Every prayer, every meal made, every gentle word, every moment of presence, every penny of generosity. Thank you for teaching me how to receive Jesus' incomprehensible love for me. — EV

table of
CONTENTS

INTRODUCTION

LITANY of WELLNESS

Lord, I praise you …

For the gift of Your creation
For my body made in Your image, in all its imperfections
For the depth of my soul and my desire for wholeness
For Your holy provision, setting me apart as Your beloved
For Your gentle love as the Good Shepherd
For sacred moments of gathering
For Your healing balm to my weary soul
For Your Holy Spirit, dwelling close and leading me to Truth

Lord, grant me the grace to see …

That You are the holy Gardener, constantly caring and tending to my unique soul
The importance of true balance of caring for my body while also tending to
my relationship with You
The ways my body might be asking for changes to be able to find balance again
Any lies that I am believing that are hindering healing in my body
The ways my choices impact not just my overall wellness,
but my relationships and the health of the generations to come

Lord, deliver me …

From my need for control over my life and my journey
From any half truths I am believing about myself and my story
From any feelings of jealousy, anger, frustration, or impatience in the face of struggle
From comparison of any others who may have walked similar paths
From viewing my greatest weaknesses alongside the greatest strengths of others
From the need to be right and attachment to any convictions not fully rooted in Your Truth

Lord, lead me, in all my days …

To dwell with You, in simplicity, peace, and joy
To live with purpose, striving for truth and goodness
To a better understanding of true health and wholeness
To have the courage to change according to Your will for me
To relinquish my need for control, with full trust in You
To revel in Your creation and its whispers of eternity
To return to You in hope, again and again

The Ember Collective is a dream that had been imprinted on our hearts for many years, and yet it took time for that dream to be spoken into reality. We have each walked a unique path that has guided us toward a love of all things holistic, wholesome, and of God. We each have encountered our own suffering as we swam in an ocean of conventionality, feeling the pull to go deeper, to further understand and support these bodies made by our Creator. This passion brought us together. Our research, professional training, and lived experience led to the birth of Ember.

The Ember Collective is a community. Centered around holistic wellness for the Catholic woman, the mission came quite naturally. Without even discussing it, we each understood that the many aspects of health and physiology we so longed to explore and share with others could only be fruitful when discussed in the context of God's provision and abundance.

Our passion project is *The Ember Journal*, a seasonal magazine to delve into incredible truths reflected in our body and the world around us. *The Ember Journal* has been in print since fall 2021. There is a plethora of content we have put out on the topics of holistic wellness, our Catholic faith, and so much in between. This book provides the perfect starting point for someone interested in these topics while offering the perfect summary for those who have been around since the beginning. The slowness and intentionality of something tactile is what led us to create a print magazine in the first place, and this is an elevation of that.

Practically speaking, it is not a simple project to translate magazine content into a book like this. Inevitably, we have left out fantastic articles that explore fascinating topics of both health and faith. This book, however, provides the foundational material upon which Ember's mission shines.

We could not start a book like this without addressing the landscape of health we find ourselves in. "Health in the 21st Century" is not an exhaustive picture across the world today, but rather a general summary of factors contributing to our modern health crises as well as the temptations of placing health as an idol. While people are facing more chronic illness today than ever before, people are also making a god out of health in more ways than we feel has previously been the case. The concise mission of The Ember Collective is *holistic wellness in light of eternity*. While we are passionate about the health of the whole person, and are often diving deep into topics of nutrition, we recognize that this life is finite and that death comes for us all. Nothing, not even good health, is worth pursuing if it is not in service of our ultimate goal: Heaven.

We then lay out a concept so fundamental to all the wellness content found in Ember: the foundations. This is the primer on topics that we consider baseline for physical health. Then we move through the seasons: living according to rhythms, big and small, handed to us by our Creator, is an intricate part of our mission. Finally, each article within the seasons has a label of either Feast, Faith, or Flourish. Feast is for all our recipes and liturgical DIYs. Faith dives into the spiritual reflections. Flourish is for those articles supporting our day-to-day integration of whole person health.

This book would not be possible without the many contributing writers who have offered their gifts and wisdom to *The Ember Journal* over the years. We thank them for their generosity — and their yes to our sharing their pieces here with you.

We are honored to create in this way, and we pray for growth and richness for all who adventure with us.

HEALTH in the 21st CENTURY

With every advancement humans have worked out, there have [generally] been positives and negatives. One side may win out in any given scenario, but all major changes have an element of something sacrificed. For instance, few people would argue that humans were better off as hunters and gatherers than they were after the agricultural revolution. That doesn't mean this major shift in civilization didn't have costs, though. This change meant less nutrient diversity and more communicable disease.

Just as our food and lifestyle habits have changed in the last 150 years, so has our environment. These changes reflect both a worsening of natural human health and resiliency, as well as a degrading of God's creation. Some of these are clear effects of sin, as we can place near direct correlations between world wars and their far-reaching impact on land, diet, and health. The reality is that, while there have been major improvements in understated areas like personal hygiene, modern day sewage and plumbing, and food safety, the past several generations have seen a worsening of foundational health. Many of the health problems today have strong connections to our environment.

Soil

There is a growing awareness for the ways the state of the soil beneath the crops affects both our health and the environment. A study published in 2024 lists the nutrient loss in high-yielding products (like apples, potatoes, and tomatoes) as up to 50 percent in the past 75 years. This is following the changes in agriculture models towards more monocropped and chemically intensive methods. Food varieties are increasingly more likely to be chosen for yield or resistance to pests over nutrient density. Nutrients, especially vital minerals like magnesium, zinc, and copper, are decreasing in value with the degradation of the soil, while toxic elements like aluminum and lead are more prevalent due to the more heavy use of chemicals. Additionally, inorganic fertilizers used in conventional agriculture run off into waterways, disturb ecosystems, and disrupt the microbiome of the soil.

The majority of cropland in America is used for corn, soy, and wheat. These are grown mainly for animal feed, the creation of things like ethanol, and to become ingredients in packaged, processed food. Glyphosate-based herbicide is routinely sprayed on all three of these crops. This is an increasingly more popular topic of conversation for concerns over its "probable" carcinogenicity to humans, negative impact on wildlife (especially pollinators), water solubility, and action as an antibiotic which can disrupt the microbiome of the soil, harm the human gut, and contribute to antibiotic resistance. Many governments around the world are legislating to ban its use over these concerns.

Heavy Metals

Heavy metals are metallic elements with high atomic weights and densities that are toxic to humans and the environment, even at low concentrations. The non-essential heavy metals (like arsenic, lead, cadmium, aluminum, and mercury) serve no function in the human body and are completely toxic. The essential heavy metals (like copper, zinc, and iron) serve vital roles, but must be bioavailable and in trace levels. Heavy metals arguably sit at the root of most common health issues today because 1) they are so much more entrenched in our food and environment than ever before, 2) they have long half-lives and are passed down in utero, causing greater issues at the start of life, and 3) they become structurally a part of our bodies, displacing important minerals. Heavy metal exposure is everywhere in our modern world, but some of the most significant sources include industrial practices, agricultural practices, and food additives.

Electromagnetic Fields (EMFs)

The topic of EMFs is a tricky and controversial one. After all, it's pretty tough to admit that those things we rely most upon in our modern life (Wi-Fi, smart phones, etc.) may be slowly and steadily harming us and our future children. To clarify, there are natural EMFs (magnetic fields from the earth's core) and there are unnatural EMFs (those created by man). While all kinds of radiation may have negative effects, it is the ionizing radiation (high frequency) that poses the most concern. Radio frequencies (wireless devices that carry information) have been classified as possibly carcinogenic by the World Health Organization and are linked to biological damage from hundreds (if not thousands) of peer-reviewed studies. We are at a point today where it is nearly impossible to live a life free of unnatural EMFs, and the best we can do is to mitigate them.

While much more could be said about the changes in our world, it suffices to understand that things have changed, and that the effects are still unraveling before us. While it doesn't serve us to hyperfocus on every harmful element around us, it would do us good to put a solid effort into educating ourselves in the foundations so that we can better care for these amazing bodies God has given us, His creation all around us, and whatever life He may put in our care.

> "The greatest merit consists in being in
> the midst of the world and yet holding
> the world under one's feet."
>
> — Jesus to St. Anne Mary Taigi

100 Years of Food Separation

The 1920 census revealed that for the first time in American history, more people were living in urban areas than rural ones. The Industrial Revolution throughout the 1800s created a momentum that changed the lifestyle of Westerners — and subsequently their health — for generations to come.

The advent of industrial milling in the late 1800s was arguably the moment when the nutrient quality of food really began to turn on its head. Now flour could be ultra-refined, filtering out the germ and pulverizing the endosperm so that it was shelf stable for months (but also lacking nutrients). After America spent decades at war throughout the early 1900s, with food needing to be sent to soldiers overseas and rationed for those at home, the consequence was an even more ultra-processed diet being "the norm." Now pile on top of that the postwar petroleum market contributing to the rise of "Big Ag" and ever-increasing production of processed vegetable oils from corn and soy — and you have the standard American diet we see today. This processed diet has been fairly consistent through the last three to four generations — and the ripple effects are now turning into waves.

In the 1930s, Dr. Francis Pottenger Jr. spent roughly ten years studying generations of cats and recorded fascinating findings about the way a mother's nutrition could ripple down through the generations that followed her. Originally built as a study on a treatment for tuberculosis, Dr. Pottenger began to notice that there was a noticeable difference in the health of the cats he was studying — depending on whether they were fed raw meat and raw milk or cooked meat and pasteurized/shelf-stable milk products. His first discovery revealed that mother cats fed a poor diet passed their physical degeneration on to their kittens over three generations, with each subsequent generation born with more and more health problems. As a child, Dr. Pottenger struggled with chronic health issues and, as a pediatric doctor, wanted to answer the question: *what if the kittens who inherited the health problems were fed a diet rich in nutrients?* He called this series of studies "regeneration." Over time he discovered that not only would a mother being fed a nutrient-rich diet benefit from better overall health, but that *each ensuing litter was healthier than the one before.*

You can't necessarily apply everything learned in an animal study to humans, but it is reasonable to assume that we have seen a similar *"ripple effect"* in the last century that is contributing to the cascade of health problems we are seeing today. Not only do we have plenty of toxins, stress, and food lacking nutrients in our environment, but so did our mothers, grandmothers, and great-grandmothers.

If mom is depleted in nutrients (especially minerals) leading up to pregnancy, during gestation, and while nursing, baby will be more likely to have less cellular energy (ATP in the mitochondria) to develop ideally, and this genetic framework will carry them through life and affect what they pass on to their children, and so on. Dr. Catherine Shanahan writes in her book *Deep Nutrition,*

> As focused as people once were on the production of healthy food, the chief crop — the ultimate prize — was the next generation of healthy children. Traditional cultures made a science of it. … Around the world, traditions reflected extensive use of special foods to boost a woman's nutrition before conception, during gestation, for nursing, and for rebuilding for the next pregnancy. Some cultures thought it prudent to fortify the groom's diet in preparation for his wedding ceremony. The shreds of surviving information suggest such knowledge was quite sophisticated. Blackfoot Nation women utilized the still-unknown nutrient systems found in the lining of the large intestine of buffalo (and later, cow) to "make the baby have a nice round head." To ensure easy delivery, many cultures reinforced preconception and pregnancy diets with fish eggs and organ meats — loaded with fat-soluble vitamins and B12 … as well as special grains carefully cultivated to be high in important minerals. The Maasai allowed couples to marry only after spending several months consuming milk from the wet season when the grass was especially lush and the milk much denser in nutrients.

Epigenetics is a growing field of study on the way our environment interacts with our genes. The field of nutrigenomics studies the interactions between diet/nutrients and the way our genes are expressed. It is becoming increasingly apparent that everything we eat, breathe, think, and even the way we move affects the way our genes are expressed. They say "genes load the gun and environment pulls the trigger" when it comes to certain genes being expressed through disease states or not.

The Lord gives each of us the blessings and crosses that we need to continually draw us back to Him, but supporting physical and spiritual health by prioritizing nourishing food, moving every day, praying every day, and creating healthy boundaries for better stress management are all choices to be prayed through intentionally.

...ARIA·GRATIA·PLENA·DOMINVS·TECVM·BENEDICTA·TV·IN·MVLIERI...

Fallen Nature

By Mackenzie Worthing

H ealing is a humbling process. It reminds us how fragile and needy we are. We often get caught up in trying to take control of our healing by exploring every available option. Maybe you are falling down a rabbit hole of information and haven't yet surfaced on the other side. Perhaps you feel frustrated that you haven't made as much progress as you had hoped. Maybe that infertility treatment didn't produce a viable pregnancy. Maybe the next therapy or chiropractor tried didn't help the child's nervous system issues. Maybe you are simply feeling overwhelmed with the vast amount of (very good!) information available about turning your lifestyle around. The availability of information on holistic healing, wellness, and true health is astounding. We should praise God to be living in this time when this information is readily available. It can also lead to information burnout, especially when you do not seem to be finding the answers you see other people getting. The intense, overpowering desire to know what is wrong with your bodily integrity or the bodily integrity of a loved one can cause its own acute sense of suffering: Why can't I heal? Why can't my baby heal? Why can't my husband heal? Why can't my mother heal? We've tried everything. We're doing everything that we can. We're exploring everything. This mindset is crippling.

The trouble is we live in a fallen world. Not only our souls were subject to the effects of original sin; the entire creation is subject to the wounds of the Fall. We are walking mysteries living in a fallen world. We have lost the beautiful, original harmony of body and soul not only in someday succumbing to death, but also in the multitudinous ways that the body can be sick, injured, dysregulated, and depleted. We can toil away at desperately clinging to health, but the fact of the matter is that health is not the highest good. Even the good, wholesome, holistic desire to live more in tune with God's design for us by healing with nutrient-dense foods, living in tune with the natural rhythm of the world, regulating the nervous system, and stocking the medicine cabinet with homeopathics and herbal remedies must be always be subordinated to the Lord's will for our lives, especially when it includes suffering. When we reject suffering, we reject the Lord's instrument of redemption. There's a balance to be struck, living in the both/and, of wanting to be healed, asking for God's blessings, doing what we can to be healthy, and also accepting that the Lord might not heal us in this life.

Those of us who are trying to reclaim the knowledge and practices of our fore-fathers when it comes to healthy living can still place health on a pedestal. Just because we love Jesus does not mean we are exempt from falling into the temptation of the modern world's emphasis on health as the highest good. It is with vivid clarity that I recall the first time I understood the implications of the "health as the highest good" mentality. I studied Rene Descartes' *Discourse on Method* in college, and in Part VI he articulates his position most clearly. After going on about how the speculative philosophy of the schools (read: theology and traditional philosophy) ought to give way to a practical philosophy (what we would consider the applied sciences) which would render men the "masters and possessors of human nature," he comes to the point that, "maintenance of health, which unquestion-ably is the first good and the foundation of all the other goods of this life, for even the mind depends so greatly on the temperament and on the disposition of the organs of the body that, if it is possible to find some means to render men generally more wise and more adroit than they have been up until now, I believe that one should look for it in medicine."

Descartes found it unquestionable that the maintenance of one's health is the first good that man must consider. He was, supposedly, a Catholic, at least for some of his life, but health was his highest good. This mentality now pervades our culture. The last few years have made this poignantly clear. The world values health above all. The world finds wisdom in the practice of medicine. There is a hunger and a thirst for knowledge in the practice of medicine unlike any other thirst for knowledge. People are willing to bend ethical questions when it comes to what can be done versus what should be done. People are willing to stake their eternal souls on their mortal bodies, subject to decay. The highest good must always and everywhere be accomplishing God's will for our lives, no matter the personal cost. The alternative is to get lost in toiling away for bodily health that will, some-day, no matter how hard we try, give way to the human condition of death. St. Paul gives us a framework in his letter to the Romans to help us put in perspective the sufferings of this life. He is a much more reliable guide for life than Descartes. He wrote more specifically about the persecutions of the early Church, yet his words can also apply to any suffering we are experiencing in this fallen world.

> I consider that the sufferings of this present time are not worth com-paring with the glory that is to be revealed to us. For the creation waits with eager longing for the revealing of the sons of God; for the creation was subjected to futility, not of its own will but by the will of him who subjected it in hope; because the creation itself will be set free from its bondage to decay and obtain the glorious liberty of the children of God. We know that the whole creation has been groaning in travail together until now; and not only the creation, but we ourselves, who have the first fruits of the Spirit, groan inwardly as we wait for adoption as sons, the redemption of our bodies. (Romans 8:18-23)

Paul points out that all of creation is subjected to futility; this applies to our persons, but also all of God's green earth. Everything that we see or experience that seems off is because nature was tainted by man's poor choice. But there is hope: all will be set free from the bondage of decay. Yet we live in a period of groaning. The whole creation groans, the sons and the daughters of the Church groan, but what are we groaning for? What are we longing for? Not only for health in this life, but the full, complete redemption of our bodies in the life to come: becoming sons of God in body and soul — the general resurrection which we profess every time we utter the Creed. Paul is sensitive to the fallen nature of man in remembering that the redemption of the world awaits. He continues, "Likewise the Spirit helps us in our weakness; for we do not know how to pray as we ought, but the Spirit himself intercedes for us with sighs too deep for words. And he who searches the hearts of men knows what is the mind of the Spirit, because the Spirit intercedes for the saints according to the will of God" (Romans 8:26-27).

We have help for our weaknesses. We do not know how to pray — we pray for all manner of things that might be a side issue to the most pressing issue of not trusting God, the quintessential problem that led to man's prideful rebellion. We have the backing of the Holy Spirit, however. We have not been left to our own devices. The Spirit will lead us back to the will of God whenever we get sidetracked or even when we willfully reject what it is He desires for our good. And He does desire our good, even when He allows us to suffer.

> We know that in everything God works for good with those who love him, who are called according to his purpose. For those whom he foreknew he also predestined to be conformed to the image of his Son, in order that he might be the first-born among many brethren. And those whom he predestined he also called; and those whom he called he also justified; and those whom he justified he also glorified. (Romans 8:28-30)

There are no caveats above. In everything, God works for our good. Do we presume to be more good, to be more merciful, to be more loving than the Lord in our plan for our lives or the lives of the ones we love? We are called according to His purpose so that we might truly become Christians, little Christs. We are being conformed to His image. Our Lord suffered greatly in His thirty-three years on earth. Why would we think that we are exempt from great suffering? We must not resist the ways in which He is trying to conform us to His image. Let us allow the Lord to work in our lives as He wills, not as we will. There is so much freedom to be found in abandoning the fallen desire to know and to do everything ourselves, even if we are attempting to apply this knowledge to good things. Let us remember that creation will be set free from its bondage to decay and that the glorious liberty of the children of God awaits us. We must not forget that we live in the time of the longing, the groaning for this to be accomplished. Let us groan then, with the Spirit, not for relief from our present sufferings but for the fulfillment of God's glorious redemption precisely through our humble submission to the will of God.

Reclaiming Our Role as Rulers with Regenerative Agriculture
by Virginia Elmer

"And he said: Let us make man to our image and likeness: and let him have dominion over the fishes of the sea, and the fowls of the air, and the beasts, and the whole earth, and every creeping creature that moveth upon the earth. And God created man to his own image: to the image of God he created him: male and female he created them. And God blessed them, saying: Increase and multiply, and fill the earth, and subdue it, and rule over the fishes of the sea, and the fowls of the air, and all living creatures that move upon the earth. And God said: Behold I have given you every herb bearing seed upon the earth, and all trees that have in themselves seed of their own kind, to be your meat: And to all beasts of the earth, and to every fowl of the air, and to all that move upon the earth, and wherein there is life, that they may have to feed upon. And it was so done."

— Genesis 1:26-30

As the health movement once again turns to animal products, realizing that the how of production matters just as much as the what, this is a perfect time for Catholics to ask themselves, What is our role in creation? *How does God want us to grow food and treat His plants and animals?*

In the garden of Eden, God assigns man with regards to creation to the role of *ruler*. As Americans who are born and bred to hate the "tyrannical crown" of monarchy, it can be difficult to understand this role as it is. But if we remove the Americanist lens (a heresy that is a conversation for another day) and see the Catholic monarch for what God intended it to be, we can very easily see our own intended role in creation. Let's take an excerpt from the renowned Catholic historian Charles Coulombe's chapter "Sacred Monarchy" in his book *Blessed Charles of Austria*:

> The new ruler took solemn oaths to uphold his realm's laws and the rights of the Church. The crown jewels bestowed upon the new monarch would often include a ring, betokening his "marriage" to his realm — it was considered to be life-long. As with both the consecration of bishops and the marriage of a couple, the union of emperor or king with empire and kingdom was held to be deep and intimate.

The picture we are left with regarding God's will for a ruler with respect to our land is a beautiful one. Land degradation or mistreatment in any way — leaving a place worse than when we found it — has no part in it, nor does letting it alone to grow to a barren wilderness. God designed plants and animals and land to be tended to, cultivated by, and improved with the work of the farmer. In a way, we enjoy a bond with the land — to protect it, to improve it, to prune back what is unhealthy, to nurture what is young.

An example of this on a microscale is livestock guardian dogs, which we use as a predator-friendly and cost-efficient way to protect our stock and gardens and allow our animals to live free-range and pastured (more on that later). Livestock guardian dogs are a unique set of breeds that have been bred over thousands of years to have a unique skill set: to be highly territorial and ward off anything encroaching their territory while at the same time developing a cross-species bond with their hoofstock and giving them precedence in their territory; to have a prey-drive that allows them to chase hawks, but leave their own chickens and poultry crawling all over and around them unharmed; to be brave enough to actively engage, fight, and destroy a predator (most dogs will back down from a fight when it comes down to it), but to use non-violent means (barking, chasing) if at all possible. If you have ever spent any time with dogs, you know these particular sets do not just happen and cannot be found in the pound. These dogs were not left to themselves to reproduce freely over thousands of years. Rather, breeders and shepherds worked hard and bred meticulously for these traits. At the same time, these dogs were not used and abused, and were not turned into something a dog cannot be. They are not miserable, aggressive creatures. Their inherent skills and tendencies as dogs were honored and cultivated into something incredibly useful.

This is, on a microscale, what regenerative agriculture attempts to do. For our family, regenerative agriculture has been the answer to how to practically be this just, benevolent ruler over the property God has entrusted to us.

Regenerative agriculture works with the design of God's creation — the "pigness of the pig" as Joel Salatin, renowned regenerative farmer, would say. We use pigs to till the ground in poor pasture, a task that they do happily. Our chickens forage for bugs, eating food they were designed to eat (chickens are not vegetarians like some marketing wants you to believe), while at the same time reducing our pest load. We companion plant our garden using a no-till, deep-mulch method to help with pests, limit the need for irrigation, avoid the use of chemical fertilizers, and let the soil microbiome flourish. Every animal and plant on our farm is here for a reason with a purpose attuned to their intelligent design by God. This is in stark contrast to the industrialized, mechanized system of conventional farming. Its sole goal is to grow as much food as possible as cheaply as possible, leading to the use of feed lots, massive poultry houses, tillers that harm the soil, and heavily applied chemical sprays. Many farmers are unaware that solutions exist that will improve their land, rather than degrade it.

Regenerative farming is the solution — it can be applied on microfarms and on a large scale. The soil is the starting point, since it (literally) feeds everything else. On our farm, our motto is "Hardy Soil. Happy Animals. Healthy Food" because a good soil houses the organisms, microbes, and minerals plants need to thrive. The animals eat the grass above it and hunt the bugs within it, eating the healthy food God created them to eat. Then we (humans) eat the plants and the animals. Whatever we can't eat is given back to the soil to be turned into compost. When we farm using regenerative methods, we know exactly what is going into our soil — and into our bodies. We cannot give what we do not have. We cannot expect to be nutritious by eating nutrient-deficient food. We cannot expect to produce nutrient-dense food on nutrient-deficient soil. A healthy soil means healthy plants, which means healthy animals who eat the plants, which means a healthy consumer who eats the animals and animal products. So, what are some basic principles we can use as farmers to return to a soil-first mentality? What are some principles we as consumers can look for in the farms we support? The methods are many and specific to the individual needs of each farm, but let's look briefly at a few common ones.

Pastured

We put our animals on fresh grass and in fresh air as soon as possible. We get the first chicks of the season in early February, and we work hard to acclimate them to cold temperatures so that they can thrive on pasture in March, even when it can still get cold. We do this because animals get more nutrients on pasture than in a barn stall or brooder. Animals raised on pasture in the sunlight absorb more vitamin D, which gives more vitamin D to us when we eat the food they produce. We say that pastured is better than organic, because commercial organic chicken can be grown in the same houses as conventional chicken, just with a few doors to an outside run with a dirt floor and room to "move." Compare that to how pastured chickens live — running through the grass picking up bugs — and it's pretty easy to see why we make that claim.

Rotational Grazing

Instead of keeping animals in one small area, rotational grazing involves intensive management by the farmer to move their animals off of their waste and onto fresh pasture, sometimes as often as daily or twice-a-day. As "ruler" of the land, the farmer takes a highly active role to maintain healthy animals, healthy forage grass, and healthy soil. The farmer ensures the animals perform just the right amount of pruning at optimal maturity for the grass and fertilizing with their waste, then lets the ground rest until it reaches optimal maturity again and they circle back, producing the healthiest grass and soil possible. Moving them off of their waste so frequently makes for much healthier animals that are less likely to deal with parasites and disease, eliminating the need to proactively treat with medication or antibiotics as is done in feed lots and conventional chicken houses.

No-Till

The soil is teeming with life below the surface. Billions of microorganisms form a soil food web made up of soil aggregates and little tunnels to transport water, oxygen, and nutrients and to make it easier for roots to penetrate. When we use our machine tillers, we disrupt these. We inject more oxygen than the system is used to. We invert the layers, moving things that like to be dark up to the light. All of this causes the immediate breakdown of organic matter, instead of the normal, slow release of organic matter over time, requiring the use of synthetic fertilizers. Is it a wonder this leaves the soil in worse shape year after year? By using no-till methods like adding compost and woodchips and planting directly into that material, we are building healthier soil with each year we plant and adding back the layers of topsoil tilling exposes and loses to erosion.

No-Spray

Something most people might not know is that chemical sprays and gardening — be it backyard hobbyist or large-scale market gardening — go hand-in-hand nowadays. Your three big enemies when trying to get something to grow from seed to leaf, fruit, or root are pests, weeds, and soil depletion. You need soil to house enough food for the plant and for insects and other plants to stay away from it. The common solution is to use three main types of chemicals: fertilizers (food for the plant), pesticides (to kill the bugs), and herbicides (to kill the weeds). However, we stay away from all three. I don't want herbicides (like glyphosate) around my family or my food because of its profound health effects. I don't want pesticides because most do not discriminate between beneficial and destructive insects. I don't want synthetic fertilizers because I don't want a bandaid solution to true soil health.

So what's a gardener to do? A soil-first mentality — building up the soil with loads of organic matter, compost we make ourselves using our pigs, and natural fertilizers from our own farm — provides enough food to make plants thrive. Methods like companion planting deter harmful insects. Weed-suppressors, like mulch and cover crops, keep plants safe from encroaching weeds. In the pasture, rotational grazing limits the need for all three of these sprays as well.

The beauty of God's design for us as stewards of a small portion of His creation is that these practices make farming something very sustainable — and not just in the political sense of the word. Farming in this way allows for someone to begin to grow their own food with little up-front cost. It is scalable, and the principles can be applied on a porch or a thousand acres. It is labor-dependent instead of machine-dependent, and the creation of jobs is much more important and sustainable than machines that break or fade into obsolescence. And, it can provide a lifetime of work for the farmer. Paul Gautschi, popular for his "back-to-Eden" method of no-till gardening, ruminates how his garden took so much work when he was younger and having to constantly build up its soil, but now he reaps the rewards of it years later, in the same garden, as an older man, with amazing soil requiring very little effort.

In fact, one could say of the conventional farming tract that one becomes more slave than ruler upon entering. Practices that leave the farmer dependent on pharmaceuticals by housing animals too close or without being rotated off of their waste make him a slave to the sickness-drug-sickness train that grows in power. Starting to farm by working for one of the big poultry companies, where you are forced to take on thousands of dollars in debt to erect massive poultry houses, enslaves you to the company protocols from the beginning. Relying on tilling in synthetic fertilizers instead of soil health is a bandaid solution that forces you to rely on more and more synthetic fertilizers each year. Much like in the health world, they fix symptoms, but not the soil, especially when the beneficial soil aggregates are broken with the industrial-sized rototiller each year.

If you want to get back to God's idea of the "rulers" of our little kingdom, it is best, as with all things, to start with ourselves. What small part of the created world is under your dominion? How can you leave it better than when you found it? It is that simple, really. Although one of my jobs is to sell food from our regenerative farm, I would much rather see my neighbors no longer in need of my products because they are doing it themselves. Can you build up soil in little pots on your balcony by composting the scraps from your kitchen? Can you support a backyard flock of a few laying hens? Can you fertilize your lawns with meat chickens instead of chemicals? Can you eliminate the Japanese beetles in your flower beds with a small flock of ducks instead of pesticides? Can you rent goats to rid your kudzu, pigs to take down your underbrush, or sheep to mow your lawn? And if you can't do these things (which might be very true, especially when I take off my rose-colored glasses for a moment), can you support someone who can?

Not only does purchasing from a regenerative farm put your money towards supporting all of these wonderful things, it can directly impact your health and the health of your family. Remember, you cannot give what you do not have — thus, supporting a farm with a soil-first mentality should mean a nutrient-dense soil, which means nutrient-dense animals and plants, which means nutrient-dense food, which means a nutrient-dense you.

When searching for your farms, look beyond the marketing labels of organic, free-range, etc. Instead, try to get to know your farmers, maybe by their social media page, chatting with them at farmers' markets or on the phone, or visiting them in person. See how they rule their little kingdoms and if they are someone you can entrust with the tremendous responsibility of growing your family's food.

"I do indeed think that suffering brings great good with it,
and like you I might wonder why any of us
should pray or labor to be delivered from it,
except that God who teaches us to take our
suffering with patience also teaches us to
pray and to do what we can to relieve our
suffering and that of our neighbor. Since
God teaches both, we need not break
our heads over the matter ...

Fasting is better than eating and brings more graces,
but God still wants us to eat. Praying is better
than drinking and much more pleasing to God,
and yet God bids us drink. Keeping vigil is more
acceptable to God than sleeping, and yet it is not
displeasing to God that we sleep ...

God has given us bodies that we might care for them
and serve him in them, until the time comes when
he takes us from this life. We cannot easily tell how
much bodily suffering we can handle, and when it
might harm our bodies or even our souls...

When God sends a storm, he expects the sailors to get
to their tackling and do the best they can for
themselves to keep the ship from going down.
So we maintain our bodies as well as we can,
and leave the degree of suffering to God. And
what we do for ourselves, we should also do
for our neighbor, with tender pity and compassion.

So it is in many cases: we call out to God in sickness and
are made whole, or in dire weather and are brought
through. We often forget our need for God in the midst
of our wealth and happiness and we cease to pray, and
God in his goodness draws us back to himself through
suffering so that he can bring his graces to us."

— St. Thomas More

The
FOUNDATIONS

Health problems can generally be boiled down to a concept of foundations and consequences. Foundations are those underlying areas of our health, often taken for granted, that should naturally work in harmony to support a healthy person: digestion, blood sugar regulation, mineral balance, etc. Consequences are the countless symptoms and diagnoses that result from one or more foundational imbalances. By understanding where the problem actually starts, we can then work to address whole-person health.

In just the last century, our quality of life as humans has largely improved. But the evolution of our environment and lifestyles seems, at times, to be incompatible with the innate needs of the human body. With chronic disease increasing at alarming rates, it is more obvious that there are missing pieces to the puzzle. Each person's path to thriving holistically is bioindividual because we each have our own set of genetics and ancestors. But it is important to look at the history of humanity as a whole, beyond just our modern Western culture.

Dr. Weston Price was a dentist from Cleveland who traveled the globe in the 1930s, studying some of the most isolated communities untouched by the western world. He was searching for the factors responsible for good dental health, mainly nutritional components. Visiting everywhere from remote villages in Switzerland to the indigenous people of Africa, the Americas, Polynesia, and Australia, Dr. Price wrote thoroughly about the diets and lifestyle of traditional people and their health. What he found were people with strong bodies, emotional stability, ease of reproduction, and freedom from degenerative ills that are considered "normal" in the modern world. These traditional people, while varied from place to place, all had nutrient-dense diets rich in fat-soluble vitamins, mainly from animal products. They understood the importance of preconception nutrition (for both parents!) and had much more room in their mouths for teeth than Dr. Price was used to seeing in America. While not everything from our hunter-gatherer ancestral diet will translate perfectly into the twenty-first century, there are foundations not to be ignored. Our stressors are different (and arguably more) and therefore sometimes warrant more intense and creative solutions. The ancestral approach is still very applicable today, essentially a matter of eating whole, unprocessed foods similar to those consumed by our ancestors. This means eating local, seasonal, and generally diverse foods (rich in animal protein), consuming nose-to-tail, and following your intuition about your unique body's needs. It's easy to get caught in the weeds in the nutrition world nowadays, but almost every state of imbalance in the body can be traced back to an imbalance at the level of the foundations of health.

"So whether you eat or drink or whatever you do,

do everything for the glory of God."

— 1 Corinthians 10:31

There is often confusion about what is meant by the phrase "properly prepared, nutrient-dense, whole foods diet." Bioindividuality — the unique needs of each person — is of utmost importance, of utmost importance, but that doesn't mean we should ignore baseline wisdom that has proven successful over countless generations.

Minimally Processed & Unrefined

The Boston Medical Journal compiled a review last year that demonstrated thirty-two specific health problems associated with the consumption of ultra-processed foods. They listed specific things like premature death, diabetes, cardiovascular disease, and mental disorders. The truth is you could probably look at any symptom and condition and find an increased risk or worsening with the consumption of ultra-processed food. This is because when we consume foods with harmful ingredients (like MSG disguised as "natural flavors," or damaging food dyes), the foundations of health are thrown off.

We can only consume a finite amount of food, and when we choose something ultra-processed, it is at the expense of a healthful choice. So instead of consuming food that will do something positive for our bodies, like adding necessary nutrients, we are opting to consume food that will cause depletions, imbalances, or direct harm.

To eat minimally processed foods means to consume either a complete whole food (such as an apple or milk) or something with entirely whole-foods ingredients (such as fermented sourdough bread or homemade mayonnaise with an olive oil base). We are not expected to be perfect, but to do our best to build our diets around real foods.

Local & In-season

There will certainly be limitations on how much we can really eat local and in-season in today's agricultural setup and economy, but the more we are able to seek this out the more benefits we will reap. Eating local not only supports the economy around you, but it means you are eating food 1) that hasn't traveled far, in a truck, exposed to potential contaminations, 2) is harvested closer to peak ripeness, meaning more nutrients, and 3) that has a diverse compilation of nutrients when done all year round. Eating in-season foods means our bodies are exposed to different nutrient profiles all year long. Not only is this wonderful for our health, but it draws us closer to God's creation and helps us to appreciate the work that goes into the production of our food.

Quality & Care

Questions we should be asking about our food (even better, at a farmers' market):
- What are the ingredients?
- What pesticides or herbicides were used in the growing of this food?
- How were these animals treated? Do they live in confined spaces/are they free to roam?
- What is the diet of the animals?

There is a lot of debate around the topic of organic food, with one of the problems being that many small farms do not have the resources to get the organic certification. This is why it is important to talk to the farmer, if possible, to gather the practices used. Many farms have higher standards than what is required for the certification, but are not allowed to label their food as organic. It's important to note that even organic farming practices use fertilizers and pesticides, but use less-processed versions. Regarding the care of animals, it is important that the livestock have room to roam on pasture, consuming their natural diet. There are so many labels on our food that say "vegetarian fed," but most animals simply need to graze on grass, bugs, etc. In some climates, there may be supplemental feed offered in harsh points of winter, but generally speaking, the diet should be from the earth.

Properly Prepared

While some foods can be eaten in their raw state (such as carrots, apples, milk), many foods need proper preparation to make them 1) digestible and/or 2) bioavailable (able to be utilized by the body). Certain nutrients are better retained in raw foods, without any cooking method applied. For instance, the fat-soluble vitamins, enzymes, and probiotics in raw milk may be destroyed or lost by high heat. Likewise, fermented and cultured foods will lose some of their probiotic content when exposed to heat.

Some nutrients, however, become more bioavailable through the cooking process and/or special preparation. The proteins in foods like meat and fish are best cooked for optimal digestion (but overcooking may denature the proteins or create dangerous compounds). Cooking certain vegetables, like onions or tomatoes, improves their nutrient profiles, making them into superfoods. Special preparation for certain foods includes the processes of soaking, sprouting, fermenting, and leavening. These are methods of traditional cultures that have been around long before the industrialization of our food system. Foods that benefit from these techniques are nuts, seeds, grains, and legumes. These processes can neutralize problematic compounds in many of these foods, thus making them easier to digest and more bioavailable.

Nutrient-Dense

Finally, we have the consideration of nutrient density. Essentially, we want to get the best bang for our buck with the food we eat. This is vastly different from calorie density. It is possible to eat a lot of "empty calories" and still be left wanting most nutrients. When people switch over from a diet high in ultra-processed foods to a diet rich in whole foods, they often don't realize that they will need to eat more to actually eat enough. Whole foods provide more nutrients, while often being lower in calories.

Additionally, it is possible to eat "clean" without eating nutrient-dense. For instance, you could have a beautiful salad with all things green. And while you may even feel full after eating a plate of these healthy foods, your body may be sorely missing out on key factors. Bioavailable protein, like grass-fed beef or wild-caught oysters, is highly nutrient-dense, containing a wide variety of macro and micro nutrients necessary for optimal health. Raw dairy can hit all of our macro needs, while boasting an impressive micronutrient profile of vitamins, minerals, enzymes, and more. This isn't to say that vegetables aren't nutrient-dense — they absolutely can be. But a meal should aim to hit many marks in a reasonable portion size. Nutrient-dense foods will always satisfy us better and fulfill our health needs more than empty calories.

A properly prepared, nutrient-dense, whole foods diet is not as complex as it seems. We just need to have eyes keen for diverse real foods that contain lots of nutrients. And when we learn to prepare meals from this base, we discover a delicious assortment that gives us energy and health.

DIGESTION

You have heard the phrase, "you are what you eat." In truth, we ought to rephrase that: *"you are what you absorb."* The mechanics of digestion function through the primary organs of our digestive tract — esophagus, stomach, small intestine, and large intestine. When digestion is functioning well, we feel good and energized after meals, we are able to fight off unwanted bacteria or pathogens that may have accompanied our food, our body breaks down macronutrients into usable compounds (amino acids, fatty acids, glucose), and it extracts nutrients which are then transported to their proper place. Basically, healthy digestion supports every system, as each system relies on nutrients. Our cells run off of nutrients; it is how we produce energy (ATP). A cursory understanding of the digestive process typically includes the stomach storing some food followed by some travels through the intestines before elimination. In reality, there are three key phases of this.

Digestion Is a North-to-South Process

If any phase is dysfunctional, it affects everything that follows. The digestion process goes as follows: Ingestion → Propulsion → Mechanical digestion → Chemical digestion → Absorption → Defecation.

The first phase of digestion is the Cephalic Phase, which precedes food even entering the stomach. The nervous system plays a major role at the very start of digestion. It is impacted by sight, smell, taste, and even thoughts. Essentially, we need to be in a parasympathetic state to digest our food: "rest and digest." It is the all-too-common "fight or flight" response that is activated, and this disrupts the entire digestion process leading to all sorts of issues downstream. Being in a parasympathetic state takes intentionality. Sitting at your desk working while mindlessly eating your lunch is a classic example of eating in a sympathetic state. You might not feel stressed, but the body perceives stress in the way of distractions. Ways to support this phase include eating away from screens, taking three to five deep breaths before eating, praying before meals, and chewing our food thoroughly. The second phase of digestion is the Gastric Phase. As we begin chewing, salivary enzymes in the mouth coat our food, beginning their work of breakdown. As the thoroughly chewed food moves to our stomach, the high acidity breaks down the proteins, does the important job of killing off unwanted pathogens, and frees nutrients to be absorbed in the intestines. Stomach acid is really the star of the show here and tends to be the downfall for most people when struggling with digestive issues. There are many factors that lead to low stomach acid (often confused for high stomach acid, funnily enough), from stress, to mineral depletions, nervous system dysfunction, or lack of nutrients. Issues like bloating, belching, heartburn, or reflux are sure signs that this phase needs support. Simple ways to support healthy stomach acid include: thoroughly chewing your food (ten to fifteen times per bite), adding digestive bitters (generally tincture form) prior to meals, drinking warm water throughout the day, avoiding a lot of liquids within thirty minutes of meals, avoiding inflammatory foods, and consuming adequate amounts of sea salt.

The Intestinal Phase

The beginning of the intestinal phase has a lot of moving parts that are easily disrupted if things *up north* didn't go so well. Once food exits the stomach, it should be broken down into macronutrients that are ready to be absorbed in the small intestine. There is a whole hormonal sequence that will be disrupted if the stomach acidity wasn't sufficient, also leading to inflammation. The presence of fat or protein in the broken-down food triggers the release of a hormone called *cholecystokinin* that slows the emptying of the stomach into the intestine, tells the gallbladder to empty its bile (from the liver) to break down fats so they can be absorbed properly, signals to the pancreas to release digestive enzymes, and tells the brain that you're starting to feel full. Our livers are workhorses, but are often pushed to the limit these days with the high-toxin, high-stress environment they're given. The liver carries out more than 500 jobs, but the main ones are to detoxify the blood and to produce bile, a substance that carries away waste and breaks down fats during digestion so that they can be absorbed properly, along with fat-soluble vitamins A, D, E, and K.

Bloating is a common symptom that can be attributed to many parts of this digestive cascade going awry, from the nervous system to insufficient stomach acid production, but where that bloating happens is in the small intestine. Either the food wasn't properly broken down by stomach acid, you're feeding bacterial overgrowth, or inflammation is occurring as a result of food sensitivities (which can be caused by overgrowth of pathogenic microbes). Ways to support this stage of digestion are through liver support, avoiding constant snacking, consuming fermented foods (if tolerated), eating quality saturated fats, staying hydrated, and sometimes supplementing digestive enzymes. You would think that since most nutrients have been absorbed by the time things get to the large intestine, there isn't a whole lot to talk about in terms of function and dysfunction at this point in the process. But that couldn't be further from the truth! Your large intestine is home to not millions or billions but *trillions* of bacterial cells, according to present research. You are a walking collection of microbes, but most of those live in your large intestine. When food is improperly broken down, those microbes may migrate northwards from the large intestine to the small intestine towards the proteins that still need need digesting. This is part of how things like small intestine bacterial overgrowth (SIBO), Candida and H. Pylori infection, and frequent bloating happen. Treatment with antibiotics can contribute to imbalances in these microbe populations as well, leading to possible tendencies for overgrowth of strains that are not beneficial for health in excess. Most of what arrives in the large intestine is indigestible fibers (to feed microbes), a small amount of bile from the liver, and water. Ideally, your body absorbs water and electrolyte minerals and the small amount of bile stimulates motility — which keeps you regular! Microbes consume what you cannot, like fibers, resistant starches, and polyphenols from plants. As microbes eat, some make short chain fatty acids like butyrate, which is used as a fuel for colon cells, is anti-inflammatory, and suppresses the activity of certain immune cells. Some microbes produce vitamins like K2 and B vitamins, which are essential to overall health. Many people experience dysfunction at this main exit point of their detoxification system, but this is almost always a result of issues upstream. Tending to your nervous system, providing diverse nutrients, and supporting your liver are all crucial to the entire process. If your liver is overburdened it will struggle to produce adequate bile to maintain colon motility. You may have motility that is too rapid, resulting in diarrhea, which can be a sign of inflammation in the large intestine. This can be caused by many things, including nutrient deficiencies, food sensitivities, small intestine bacterial overgrowth, or histamine intolerance.

Foods that are most likely to cause dysbiosis in your gut microbiome are things like processed carbs and large amounts of antimicrobial fatty acids like linoleic — a polyunsaturated fat found in vegetable oils that are used in many processed foods. Other microbiome disruptors are things like chlorine, antimicrobial soaps and sanitizers, food/beauty product preservatives, pesticides/herbicides, and overuse of antibiotics. One of the best ways to support your large intestine is to support everything *north* of it in the digestion process, but there are also ways to support the microbes there. These include nervous system support, a diverse diet, prebiotic-rich foods, probiotic-rich foods (if tolerated), and getting outside. *As always, if you have concerning symptoms please consult your doctor.*

BLOOD SUGAR

Blood-sugar regulation is one of the core foundations of health and is the process by which the body maintains a narrow range of blood glucose (blood sugar). Our cells' preferred source of energy is glucose, so it is hugely important to nourish ourselves with this in mind. Blood-sugar regulation is controlled by the central nervous system and its communication with several organs (pancreas, adrenals, adipose tissue, liver, and skeletal muscle). It is so important for our survival that the body tightly regulates these levels to maintain homeostasis (similar to body temperature). There are natural ebbs and flows to our blood-sugar levels throughout the day. It is natural for it to rise and fall, which is not a concern. It becomes a concern when it is commonly outside of a healthy range. Very simply put, when blood sugar is too high, the pancreas releases insulin to bring glucose into the cells. When blood sugar dips too low, the pancreas releases glucagon which brings stored glucose into the bloodstream. This can all happen quite harmoniously when we nourish ourselves and manage stress properly, with the other organs performing their duties as well. When we rely too much on the body to bring us back into balance without cultivating good habits to support blood-sugar, organs begin acting in a manner of survival, harming long-term health. The consequences of blood-sugar imbalances are numerous, but often show up in our hormones, sleep, mood, and immune health, to name a few. While some of the consequences are quite serious, simple steps taken to address blood-sugar regulation can lead to profound improvement in symptoms (though this may take some time). Common symptoms associated with blood-sugar issues include: frequently waking up at night (particularly in between one and four a.m.), consistently having little to no appetite for breakfast, craving sweets after meals, afternoon fatigue, excessively frequent urination, hormonal imbalances, weight issues, relying on stimulants for energy, addiction to busyness or stress, or being unable to go three to four hours between meals.

Basic Blood Sugar Supports

- Pair protein and carbohydrates together at every meal/snack.
- Eat every three to four hours (some people need to eat every two to three hours).
- Eat within thirty to sixty minutes of waking and sixty minutes before bed.
- Focus on nutrient density with priorities on minerals.
- Consume animal-based protein and easy-to-digest whole-food carbohydrates.
- Eat enough nutrient-dense foods.
- Hydrate with mineral-rich drinks.
- Drink coffee only after a nourishing breakfast.
- Begin your day with a savory breakfast, rich in protein (thirty-plus grams).
- Make walking a part of your daily rhythm, especially after a large meal.
- Incorporate strength training into your exercise routine.

Blood Sugar "Hacks"

Below are tips that can help manage blood sugar in instances when our circumstances aren't ideal or conducive to healthy blood sugar.

- Consume one to two teaspoons of vinegar about thirty minutes before meals.
- If breakfast is going to be more than an hour after waking, drink water (you can add a splash of juice if you prefer) with a scoop of protein powder, with a small side of fruit.
- Eat the food on your plate in this order: veggies (fiber), protein/fat, starches, then sugars.
- Activate your calf muscles within ten to twenty minutes after a meal.
- Save any dessert for after a full meal.
- Drink chamomile tea after a carb-heavy meal.

MINERALS

Minerals are inorganic substances not made by living organisms. There are many known minerals, but only some of them are required by the body. They come from the earth — they are the ash that remains when plants or animal tissues are burned. While some vitamins can be made by the body, all minerals we need must be consumed through food and drink.

Minerals Are the Spark Plugs of the Body

What do we mean when we say "spark plugs?" Minerals ...
- Are cofactors in enzymatic reactions.
- Regulate pH of blood.
- Facilitate transfer of nutrients in/out of cells.
- Maintain proper nerve conduction.
- Help control contracting and relaxing muscles.
- Regulate tissue growth.
- Provide structural and functional support.

They are required to get enzymatic reactions going. Without adequate minerals, there is nothing to "spark" the reactions we all need to function. It then follows that minerals are essential for the body to make hormones and equally necessary for vitamins to do their jobs, particularly the fat-soluble vitamins A, D, E, and K. While there are countless vitamin supplements on the market, the industry often fails to capture the real issue, which is often mineral status. When speaking of minerals, it's imperative we focus on balance. Having sufficient amounts is important, but when addressing a mineral issue (which is a foundational issue) it's more likely an imbalance. Minerals are synergistic and antagonistic. For instance, calcium and magnesium need each other, but they also oppose each other. And while calcium levels may sometimes seem exceedingly high, it might not be due to dietary calcium as much as a deficiency in other necessary factors.

Minerals are broken down into macrominerals (those found in larger amounts in the body) and trace minerals. This simply helps us understand which minerals are found in more abundance in the body — naturally drawing our attention, but that's not to say any minerals are less important. Anytime we look at mineral balance in the body, we always look to four primary minerals first: calcium (Ca), magnesium (Mg), sodium (Na), and potassium (K). Once you fully grasp how important the metabolism is for overall health and its impact on bodily resiliency, investing in mineral balance is a natural progression.

WATER

There is something undeniably healing to the soul that comes with sitting near a fresh babbling brook or plunging waterfall. The sound of ocean waves is one of the most relaxing in the world, and the most idyllic destination vacations are often beautiful locations near water. Water makes up so much of our world and so much of us. It is something we can't neglect when speaking about health — or our good Lord's creation and its balm for our weary souls! In fact, water is our largest macronutrient, essential to life. Water delivers nutrients to our cells and improves the communication between them. Water also creates environments that physically rebalance our bodies in terms of electrical charge — think waterfalls and ocean waves!

The quality of the water you drink greatly impacts proper hydration and mineral balance. Electrolytes like sodium, magnesium, and potassium (to name a few) enhance the body's ability to utilize water. Unfortunately, the quality of tap water and most bottled water is sub-par, as part of its processing leads it to contain contaminants like heavy metals, industrial chemicals, synthetic fertilizers, or harmful elements like chlorine and fluoride. Water is actually a complex substance, containing hundreds of naturally occurring minerals and chemicals. Some filtration methods like reverse osmosis or distillation not only filter out contaminants, but also strip the water of vital minerals. This "thirsty" water will not support proper mineral balance and hydration and will actually lead to greater dehydration and toxicities over time since the body relies on mineral-rich water for so much of its balance. Spring water is best if it can be sourced well, as it will contain natural ratios of minerals and elements. The bottom line of filtration is that it is unique to *your* home and location and needs to be assessed as such.

In terms of water in our environment, the water in our bodies is affected by electrical charge. Ions are molecules floating in the air that have gained or lost an electrical charge, becoming either positive or negative. These ions have chemical reactions with your bodily tissues. Positive ions are found in things like pollution, dust, toxic chemicals, mold, and EMFs generated from phones, computers, etc. Negative ions exist in nature in the electricity of a lightning storm, sunlight, wherever water collides with itself (waterfalls and ocean waves), in growing plants, even in burning beeswax candles. There is a reason that waterfalls and lush forests are calming! Grounding (or *"earthing"*) is the practice of planting your bare feet on the earth, which abounds with negative ions. The earth is a natural conductor, as are all living things. Negative ions make you feel rested and rejuvenated, so it is in favor of our health to seek them out! You could take a hike through a lush forest (or just your neighborhood!), slip your shoes off outside, dip your toes in fresh water, get your hands in the soil, or just soak up some sunshine.

SLEEP

Sleep is simple, right? It is a universal human function and need. You might wake up looking forward to your next slumber, or you might avoid it at all costs. Either way, all succumb to it. We literally cannot survive without it. But it's not just because it's restful or that it simply helps us bridge one day to the next. God ordained sleep as an inescapable part of our lives for many reasons, both physical and spiritual. There is much to be said on the spirituality of sleep, but for this brief introduction we will focus on the most important physical functions.

Dr. Matthew Walker, Founder and Director of the Center for Human Sleep Science, claims, "Every physiological system in the body and every single operation of the mind is enhanced by sleep when you get it and demonstrably impaired when you don't get enough." Insufficient sleep, he suggests, can also be linked to nearly every disease of the developed world. Lack of sleep in the short-term does not just affect you in the here and now, but can contribute to a host of long-term health issues. The old adage, "I'll sleep when I'm dead" is not wisdom you want to heed.

It's always important to view health in context, and sleep is a big part of the picture. At the end of the day (say, 10 p.m.?), there is only so much that solid nutritional habits can do for you if your body is unable to restore through sleep. So what is actually happening when we sleep? Why is it so vital? Sleep is a complex state dependent upon many processes in the body and relying on a healthy metabolism. The restoration that occurs heavily revolves around detoxification. Without the ability to properly detoxify, countless mechanisms in the body suffer. Some of the body's priorities during sleep include:

- ***Brain processing, memory formation, and consolidation:*** These hugely important functions greatly impact our ability to learn and make memories.

- ***Stress relief:*** Darkness signals stress to the body, so we naturally crave sleep at night as a protection against that stress. Considering our ancestral roots as well, nighttime was the perfect time to settle in as a group and rest away from the danger of predators.

- ***Tissue healing and growth:*** While the body is at rest in most places, it can afford to use energy on those less-urgent but highly vital processes like healing.

- Immune system function: I think everyone innately understands the importance of sleep to our immune system; it's something we all naturally gravitate towards when ill. Immune-cell activity is higher during sleep, aiding in the recovery process.

- Brain detoxification: Cells produce energy, but they also produce waste. During sleep, the body is able to take the time to escort that waste.

Support Better Sleep

- Balance Blood Sugar: This is something that needs to be cultivated every day and one of the most foundational things we can do to optimize our sleep. By eating every three to four hours, combining protein and carbs at each meal/snack, and focusing on nutrient-dense, mineral-rich food sources, we can help prevent unnecessary stress responses which have negative effects all day and night long.

- Consume a bedtime snack: Not just any kind of snack; we want it to be the right support. Components of a good bedtime snack include: (1) sodium (salt), which reduces stress mediators that can increase during sleep; (2) glucose from something simple like honey, fresh fruit, or milk; (3) protein, which helps improve the insulin response from the carbohydrates. Best protein sources include bone broth, collagen, gelatin, and milk.

- Check your light: Most of us are exposed to an abundance of artificial light during the day, which has a number of detrimental effects including disruption of our circadian rhythm. The best ways to counteract this and to restore that rhythm while at the same time improving the metabolism is to increase exposure to natural light. The easiest way to do this is by getting outside and enjoying actual sunlight. But sometimes that's not always easy, so adding in red light therapy (or at least an amber light bulb in a lamp used in the evening) can be a wonderful support.

- Avoid screens before bed: This goes hand in hand with light, but to optimize sleep and support our circadian rhythm, it's best to part with screens at least an hour or two before bed. If that's not possible, consider investing in some blue-light-blocking glasses or software.

"God is there in these moments of rest and can give
us, in a single instant, exactly what we need. Then
the rest of the day can take its course, under the
same effort and strain, perhaps, but in peace.

And when night comes and you look back over the
day and see how fragmentary everything has been
and how much you planned that has gone undone
and all the reasons you have to be embarrassed and
ashamed: just take everything, exactly as it is, put it in
God's hands and leave it with Him. Then you will be
able to rest in Him — really rest — and start the next
day, as a new life."

— St. Edith Stein

TOXINS

Toxins can be anything that is irritating or harmful to the body. Any substance can be a "toxin" in excess — even water, sodium, or any nutrient. The body has an efficient and complex detoxification system that is capable of removing toxins. Problems arise when the toxic load becomes too much. If we are exposed to too many toxins in excess, the body may not be able to process it all. Your body will prioritize survival and will remove toxins from the bloodstream and store them in our tissues if necessary. This is a GOOD thing because it protects us from immediate harm, but if not addressed, it causes long-term health problems.

> Toxins enter our bodies every day through the food we eat, the water we drink, the air we breathe, the substances we touch or apply to our faces and bodies — even the drugs prescribed by doctors and dentists. Until you reflect upon all that you take in without a second thought, the many ways you are exposed to toxins may seem hidden and surprising.
>
> — Dr. Joseph Pizzorno, *The Toxin Solution*

The Toxic Burden

Many of us are BORN with a toxic burden that has already overloaded us. This is contributed to by mama's existing toxic load, drugs/medical interventions during pregnancy, and poor nutrition in the generations preceding us. In 2004, The Environmental Working Group spearheaded a study on the amount of toxins in the umbilical cord blood of ten babies. The results showed more than 200 toxins including pesticides, carcinogens, and toxins harmful to development and neurological health.

From day one, our broken world provides an onslaught of burden to our detoxification system. The standard diet nowadays includes its own cocktail — glyphosate, food dyes and additives, MSG, artificial sweeteners, etc. Chemicals in our cleaning and hygiene products are often questionable in terms of harm to our health. It gives a little perspective to hear that in Europe, more than 1,000 chemicals are banned from cosmetics and in the U.S. it's a number more like ten. Medical interventions and procedures, such as amalgam fillings, have long-term effects that are still not fully known. Some people live in environments with a high mycotoxin load from mold that can also have detrimental effects on health.

The Drainage Funnel

Nutrients and waste must be able to move freely in the body to be absorbed and disposed of properly. This "drainage funnel" is the sum of the body's natural processes to eliminate toxins.

1. Cells: Our mitochondria are the powerhouses of our cells, where ATP (energy) is created. Healthy mitochondria are necessary for this process, but are also needed to detoxify.

2. Organs/Tissues: It is important we support the brain's ability to detox through the glymphatic system, a waste clearance system that ultimately helps with the elimination of neurotoxic waste. This only happens while we sleep, so prioritizing sleep is of utmost importance.

3. Lymphatic System: Lymph flows through lymph nodes where bacteria, viruses, and organic material are filtered out. It acts like a pre-filter for the liver (so as to not cause overload). Lymph needs our help to get moving.

4. Liver & Bile Ducts: The liver filters toxins from the blood and neutralizes them in prep for elimination. These neutralized toxins pass to the gallbladder in bile and are eventually excreted in feces. If the liver and bile ducts are clogged, toxic bile acids may make their way to other organs (skin, lungs, kidneys) through the bloodstream.

5. Colon: If you're not having bowel movements regularly (minimum once/day), your colon is not assisting in the detoxification process properly and toxins can become stagnant in the body. The state of the nervous system, hormones, mineral balance, hydration, and microbiome all play a part in this.

When the "Bucket" Topples Over

Each of us have our own "bucket" of a toxic load to deal with. Our body is created to be capable of dealing with this, but problems arise when it becomes too much for the system to handle and things stop working properly. If we don't provide our bodies with the necessary nutrients and cofactors, the detoxification system is more likely to struggle. It's also important to remember that the liver metabolizes hormones as well as toxins, so if we are dealing with chronically elevated cortisol and dysregulated blood sugar, this will contribute to the "bucket." A diet lacking in minerals burdens the body, especially the kidneys, which are a crucial part of our detoxification system. Poor fat digestion clogs the lymph and the liver, and not enough protein (or the right kinds of proteins/amino acids) hinders the liver's detox pathways.

There are many people today who are living with an incredible toxic burden, but the body has been preserving them by moving everything out of direct harm's way and/or placing the immune system into hyperactive mode. These people will still have symptoms (high blood pressure, weight gain/inability to lose weight, fatigue, poor/hyperactive/suppressed immune systems), but can press on until the body reaches its breaking point. When we start supporting drainage, providing the body with the right nutrients, and removing especially harmful things, symptoms may get worse. This is the strange thing about healing. Things often get worse before they get better. The body is finally releasing things it's held on to, sometimes for decades: heavy metals, excess minerals or recycled hormones, harmful bacteria and pathogens, and even trauma (which actually gets stored in our cells!). This can be an uncomfortable time that pushes people back to old, comfortable habits. But healing is not a linear process, and this is where working with an experienced practitioner can make all the difference.

Why Stir Things Up If It Will Make Me Feel Worse?

We are the culmination of a few generations with less-than-ideal environments. Our toxic exposures continue to grow; even for those who have taken measures to mitigate these stressors, many of us are working with a full bucket that we've inherited. Not everyone will experience obvious symptoms at a young age, but there is more and more evidence linking toxins to all sorts of diseases. Heavy-metal toxicity has strong associations with many conditions from autism to Alzheimer's, conventional dentistry has correlations with breast cancer, EMFs may be contributing to various cancers (even in children) — the list goes on. While it can be hard to pinpoint the exact causes to these ailments (it will vary from person to person), it is clear that the general environment (and toxins that come along with it) we are living in today is not leading to an improvement in the general public's health, but a degradation of it. If you are (or have yet to be) in your childbearing years, this adds another layer of importance to evaluating our environment. Processed food — though a big factor — is not the only thing threatening the health of our children. The smaller a person is (and a nine-week-old baby in utero is pretty small!), the more adversely affected they are by harmful substances. *Conversely, they may respond much quicker to healing.*

Aside from physical disease, toxins affect our mental state on a day-to-day basis. When the body (and mind) cannot process something — be it a toxin, emotion, or whatever — it can breed major imbalances. An unhealthy liver is associated with anger, unhealthy cells and tissues store trauma, and pathogens in the gut will feed off of neurotransmitters leading to anxiety and depression. When it comes to detoxing heavy metals, the most basic and effective strategy (aside from eliminating the source if possible) is mineral balance. Heavy metals compete with minerals in the body, but if we are able to increase our mineral stores and achieve balance, then the heavy metals are more likely to be eliminated, assuming drainage pathways are open. For instance, Chlorine, Fluoride, and Bromine compete with Iodine, blocking iodine receptors in the body. Iodine is needed to make thyroid hormone, so when we are overloaded with these other toxins (and not getting enough iodine from our diet), our thyroid and metabolic health suffer.

Looking Ahead

While the prospects of good health may seem bleak when reflecting on a topic as vast as this, it's important to know this: we will never be able to rid our life of every toxin. That may seem like the nail in the coffin, but it's actually meant to lessen this mental burden. No matter how many actions we take to mitigate the harms around us, they will always be there. So there is absolutely no point stressing about it. One of the factors that actually improves our physical response to toxins is our mental state and resilience to stress. When it comes to perspective and mentality: Are you obsessing? Are you overly scrupulous with what you allow into your life? Do you let it negatively impact your closest relationships? Does fear prevent you from moving forward? Then thinking about resiliency: Do you eat a nutrient-dense diet? Do you get outside daily? Do you prioritize healthy relationships? Do you trust in the hand of God? All of these affect how our body processes those things that don't contribute to our good. Finally, on a hopeful note, the human body is capable of wonderful things. While we may be around the low point of genetic wealth, it has taken generations to get here. However, through intentionally nurturing the health of our whole person, by eating nutrient-dense, whole foods that work with our body, by placing the first things first and allowing Providence to joyfully reign in our lives, we have the opportunity to cooperate in the creation of healthier generations to come.

"May the Lord give you increase, you and your children."

— Psalm 114:15

Helpful Supports for Detoxification (from cells to colon)

- Hydration
- Mineral balance
- Sauna therapy
- Quality sleep
- Deep breathing
- Dry brushing
- Castor oil packs
- Adequate protein
- Coffee enemas
- Raw carrot salad
- Therapeutic massages
- Digestive bitters
- Spore-based probiotics
- Liver-supporting herbs (milk thistle, dandelion root, etc.)
- Liver-supporting foods (beets, well-cooked cruciferous veggies, etc.)
- Gentle movement (walking, rebounding)

MOVEMENT

by Anna Truxillo

Nutrition, as most are aware, represents a standard staple for health, and as the ever-revolving door of diets linger in society, movement is often forgotten about. Quality movement is essential for improving balance, coordination, posture, joint and bone health, overall strength, and metabolic health, just as nourishing our bodies with appropriate foods can be.

> "The paradox of the modern world is this: Not only do we do less, physically,
>
> than ever before, but we also almost never do nothing."
>
> — Katy Bowman, *Move Your DNA*

However, there's a catch: not all types of exercise yield the same benefits. Aerobic, endurance exercise (like cardio-based workouts) increase the heart rate and breathing rate continuously for a certain amount of time, but actually work against the body when it comes to improving our metabolic rate, muscle production, and fat loss.

Here's how: During intense exercise or long, steady state cardio, we become breathless and begin to mouth breathe, releasing too much CO_2 in relation to O_2. Without adequate CO_2 levels, the body will break down glucose for energy without oxygen, and the byproduct of this process is lactic acid. The muscles will then begin to take up water and swell in response to lack of oxygen and stress, incidentally leading to soreness and tightness. Persistent, intense or endurance exercise leads to a lack of oxygen, increased adrenaline, rapid heart rate, a breakdown of muscles for energy, and increased levels of stress hormones and lactic acid, and the body will actually down-regulate the metabolism in response, leading to a harder time burning fat. Does this mean we should never do aerobic or cardio exercise? Not necessarily, but we must take into account our personal stress levels, goals, and overall health before diving into these endurance workouts. Are there better options when it comes to getting the most "bang for your buck" in regards to the benefits of exercise? Yes!

> "Different types of exercise have been identified as destructive or reparative
>
> to the mitochondria; 'concentric' muscular work is said to be restorative to
>
> the mitochondria. Concentric resistance training has an anabolic effect
>
> on the whole body."
>
> — *Ray Peat*

Anaerobic exercise involves short bursts of intense physical activity with rest in between, such as strength training. Concentric muscular exercise, or exercise that causes the muscle to contract against resistance, increases carbon dioxide and circulation. Resistance training also increases strength and muscle mass, and increased muscle is beneficial for not just your musculoskeletal system, but also your metabolism. Muscle is a metabolically active tissue, which means it burns more calories at rest than fat does. Therefore gaining muscle will make your ability to burn fat easier as you are increasing the amount of metabolically active tissue in the body. While resistance training is preferred, you can still push yourself beyond your "metabolic threshold," which simply means you progressed past the point where your body could effectively mitigate the stress from the workout and instead have caused the body to compensate. We often associate extreme soreness with the workout "working," however, this is one sign that the body is stressed during the workout and having trouble repairing thereafter.

Using your ability to maintain nasal breathing can lead to a better understanding of the intensity of workouts your body can manage. According to Dan Brulé from Just Breathe, "Studies show that you can reduce your heart rate, blood pressure, and cortisol levels by up to 20%" through nasal breathing. Your breathing is the key to recovery and will be your movement guide. Diaphragmatic breathing also strengthens the diaphragm and pelvic floor, and improves posture. If you find yourself becoming breathless and unable to keep a steady inhale and exhale through the nose during the workout, you may need to rethink the intensity of your training or how you are fueling your workout.

Take your movement sessions beyond simply walking, squatting, and bicep curls, and opt for functional movement training. Returning to more complex movement patterns, or Primal Movement Patterns (squat, bend, lunge, push, pull, twist, and gait) as coined by physiologist Paul Chek, offers not only increased strength and muscle mass from resistance training, but also focuses on the movement patterns our bodies are designed to do - patterns we actually perform daily. Therefore, becoming stronger in these movement patterns will lead to greater carryover in our daily life, hence the phrase "functional movement." It also greatly challenges the brain, further stimulating the metabolism, as an active brain consumes a tremendous amount of fuel!

Contrary to popular belief, you don't need to spend hours in the gym to get results. Instead, just three sessions of thirty minutes of functional strength training per week will yield great results, as long as you are challenging yourself, fueling the body, and emphasizing proper recovery through breath, rest, and nourishment.

"Perhaps the only way out of our poor physical state, created by our culture of convenience, is a return to the behaviors of our ancestors."

— Katy Bowman

PART TWO

LIVING the SEASONS

SPRING

As Catholics, we know that miracles happen. The Gospels are full of miracles performed by Jesus. But miracles are not simply reserved for Scripture — God intervenes still today. The word "miracle" gets thrown around a lot — childbirth, an event beyond our expectations, a long-awaited conversion of a loved one. But a miracle is a supernatural sign that occurs in our natural world. Even when in harmony with nature's potential (for instance, a very ill person's potential for good health), miracles bypass what would be the normal process. The primary purpose of a miracle is to glorify God and to draw people to Him. These experiences are not able to be explained by science and have their root in God's direct intervention.

And then there are wonders — experiences of healing witnessed in more hidden spaces: the gradual, but long-hoped-for healing of chronic illness, a healthy pregnancy after years of infertility, a child coming back to the faith. These may go unnoticed by the world, but have the potential to be pivotal moments in the faith journeys of individuals, families, and communities. They help to reveal the beauty and intricacy with which we were made. We should absolutely celebrate these wonders — and not let the opportunity to glorify God go to waste. And while it may be simple to explain away these wonders with our human effort and work, God is the divine physician and "in all things God works for good with those who love him" (Romans 8:28). All glory be to Him alone.

Spring is a time for hope. The world around us awakens, while our souls are stirred through Lent to new life at Easter. As we age, it can be easy to lose the gift of wonder so innate to a child. But the gift of wonder not only helps us to really see God at work, but also inspires us to have the proper awe and reverence for it all. If you've felt like the gift of wonder has evaded you for some time, pray for it. Pray to become like a child, to wonder at the mysteries and goodness all around you — never ceasing to give glory to God.

"Behold, I make all things new. "

— Revelation 21:5

spring

EMBER DAYS

"I am the light of the world; he who follows me
will not walk in darkness, but will have eternal life."

—John 8:12

The Ember Days are four sets of three days throughout the liturgical year where Catholics were traditionally called to prayer, fasting, and almsgiving in preparation for the upcoming season. While no longer required throughout dioceses in the US, many still incorporate this practice today.

Wednesday: fasting and partial abstinence
Friday: fasting and full abstinence
Saturday: fasting and partial abstinence

**fasting: one full meal and two smaller meals/snacks*
**partial abstinence: meat at one meal is allowed*
**full abstinence: no meat is permitted*

The spring Ember Days, or Lenten Embertide, takes place during the first week of Lent following Ash Wednesday. We give thanks for the rebirth of nature and for the gift of light. We can particularly call to mind flowers and bees that help make the candles for sacramental use. While we pray materially for God's blessing for a fruitful harvest, we should pray also for priests and seminarians. "The harvest is plentiful but the workers are few. Ask the Lord of the harvest, therefore, to send out workers into his harvest field" (Matthew 9:37-38).

"We beseech Thee, O Lord, illumine our minds with the
light of Thy brightness: that we may see what has to be
done and have the strength to do it."

— Prayer over the people for Ember Wednesday in Lent

what's in season?
SPRING

Vegetables

- Asparagus
- Mushrooms
- Arugula
- Beets
- Collard greens
- Parsnips
- Swiss chard
- Chives
- Lettuce
- Onions
- Radishes
- Kohlrabi
- Spinach
- Carrots

Fruits

- Apricots
- Grapefruit
- Lemons
- Pineapple
- Mango
- Rhubarb
- Strawberries
- Cherries

We sometimes forget, as a culture that can head to the grocery store and pick up any fruit or vegetable we want for most of the year, that nature has an ebb and flow to her harvests. In the very first days of your spring farmers' market, the greening of spring will be on display — lettuces, spinach, radishes, kohlrabies, snap peas. All of this green lends itself to cleansing the body after a long winter. After a couple of months, this will give way to more cucumbers, zucchinis, strawberries, green beans, and potatoes to provide ample nutrient-rich carbohydrates for the busy summer ahead. And following that are the heat-loving summer crops like tomatoes, peppers, melons, okra, and an abundance of fresh, mineral-rich, hydrating fruits for the heat of the year! And then come the more hearty root vegetables and warming spices and other foods of autumn into winter. The beauty of consuming fresh foods that are in season is evident in the abundance of vitamins and minerals they contain when picked at the proper time as opposed to, say, buying strawberries at the grocery store in the dead of winter. Those out-of-season foods are often harvested before they are ripe and travel thousands of miles to your table. Not only do our wallets thank us for prioritizing seasonal produce, but it also is one of the ways we can participate in the beauty of the seasons.

FASTING

"Fasting gives birth to prophets and strengthens the powerful; fasting makes

lawgivers wise. Fasting is a good safeguard for the soul, a steadfast companion for

the body, a weapon for the valiant, and a gymnasium for athletes. Fasting repels

temptations, anoints unto piety; it is the comrade of watchfulness and the artificer of

chastity. In war it fights bravely, in peace it teaches stillness."

— St. Basil the Great

Fasting is an ancient practice that predates the Church and is seen throughout the Old Testament in conjunction with prayer. This practice is emphasized throughout the Gospels, integrating it with the life of a Christian. The Church has always placed special importance on fasting alongside prayer and almsgiving (*CCC* 1534). Fasting, with a spirit of self-denial, is an indispensable part of the Christian spiritual life. With a heart properly oriented, fasting is spiritually fruitful and in some instances is our best weapon in spiritual battle. In two different Gospels, we see a boy, possessed by a demon, was brought to the disciples and they were unable to heal him. When they asked Jesus why, He replied, "This kind is not cast out but by prayer and fasting" (Matthew 17:20).

The Church calls us to a true fast on only a handful of specific days throughout the year. But as we grow in our faith, we may feel drawn (or advised by a priest or spiritual director) to fast in a more substantial way. Many of us have had the realization in our own lives that certain intentions will require more of us: for radical conversions to the faith of loved ones, peace and deliverance for those under persecution, preparation for difficult conversations or situations, or working to root out habitual sin. These are a few examples of times when fasting is often considered, alongside fervent prayer and almsgiving.

Spiritual Benefits of Fasting

It is evident that fasting can be immensely fruitful. When considering the purposes we fast, St. Thomas Aquinas mentions three: (1) to restrain the desires of the flesh; (2) to raise the mind to contemplate sublime things; and (3) to make satisfaction for our sins (*Summa Theologica* II). Fasting helps us to grow in the virtue of temperance, or self-control. By restraining ourselves from the desires of the flesh, we strengthen our spiritual muscles, which in turn helps build a sturdier defense against other temptations. When we are able to abstain from earthly things (even if they are good), we also make more space for the Lord. This allows our focus to shift from "self" to God, and consequently to others.

> "For if you live according to the flesh, you will die, but if by
> the spirit you put to death the deeds of the body, you will live."
>
> — Romans 8:13

Finally, fasting is a way we can make reparation, either for our sins or the sins of others. While absolution in sacramental Confession means we are forgiven of our sins — and penance is a part of reparation — "Every offense committed against justice and truth entails the duty of reparation, even if its author has been forgiven" (CCC 2487). The most perfect way to offer reparation is through the holy sacrifice of the Mass, and sometimes reparation is material. Fasting, however, is another means for repairing damage done through sin.

Fasting and Health

Fasting and a spirit of self-denial are integral to the Faith. Fasting as a health trend is a bit more complicated. And when we begin to mix the two ideas, thinking that our fasting on Good Friday is at the same time offering us health benefits, things can get murky. Sure, humans have fasted throughout all of human history, but almost always (outside the context of religion) it was simply out of survival and necessity. Our ancestors had a degree of metabolic flexibility, which allowed them to survive with sporadic eating patterns. Men, more so than women, are more innately built for this since they would be the ones gone for long periods of time hunting or fulfilling other duties. These people also lived close to creation, in the sense that nourishment was dependent on their location and season. So while food may have been more scarce in winter, they naturally stored up certain nutrients in seasons prior.

This way of living could not be further from what we experience today. For starters, we are not living nearly as close to nature, despite the great efforts of some. This isn't de facto a bad thing (it offers many benefits our ancestors did not have), but is just a function of the time we live in. The bigger factor, however, is stress. The greatest stressors on our ancestors would have likely been an acute stress — a predator or a lack of food. This is not to trivialize their lives or say that they were easy (far from it!), but people today are quite literally born with stress. As we grow, the stressors compound — long school days at a young age, positive or negative pressure from peers or parents, chronic illness, medical interventions, unhealthy relationships, financial burdens, job insecurity, lack of authentic community, poor nutrition, environmental factors (water quality, EMFs, mold, etc.). The list could go on and on. The point being that while our biology has not evolved that much, the world in which we are living has changed drastically, which has resulted in our bodies being immensely stressed (even when we don't "feel" it). So while our ancestors may have been able to get by with "intermittent" fasting, most people today are not equipped for that kind of demand on the body. An overnight fast is sufficient for most people to reset digestion among a few other things.

There are plenty of studies showing potential health benefits of [intermittent] fasting, including weight loss, improved metabolic health, cellular regeneration, and more. The thing is, you can find (or create) a study to support almost anything. And with nearly any "diet" or approach to eating, one can see immediate "results." Long-term fasting, especially for women of child-bearing age, is a stress on the body. Stress hormones take over, which can explain some of the immediate returns (because running on stress hormones can feel good). Our liver is especially compromised, as this vital organ needs regular, consistent fueling to do its many jobs. Long-term fasting doesn't typically address any root cause, but can lead to a great deal of dysregulation. Of course everyone is bioindividual, and it would be wrong to say that it is never appropriate for every person. However, it would not be on the short list of things to consider when evaluating health approaches.

God First

But does that mean that we should be hesitant to fast for religious reasons? No. It is partly because fasting is difficult on the body that it has so much spiritual significance. As St. Thomas Aquinas writes, "Fasting means not only abstaining from superfluity of food, but also from what is necessary." Food is a necessity. A true fast requires more than saying no to treats (desserts and alcohol being prime examples). A true fast comes at a true cost. It asks us to do something contrary to our nature, to deny ourselves something we need, and to offer up the sacrifice of that unfulfilled need to God.

If we are of the mindset, though, that our sacrifice is also benefiting us physically, it can distort our intentions, even if we are doing our best to be true. It is not uncommon to see people doing diets for Lent, or giving up foods in an attempt at weight loss, or adding practices that will strengthen the body. While none of this is inherently wrong, we must honestly ask ourselves if our primary intention is to serve God. Fasting relies on supernatural grace to overcome our physiological wants AND needs. St. Francis de Sales writes,

> For if I fasted chiefly in order to save money, rather than from obedience to the Church; if to study well rather than to please God — who does not see that I pervert right and order, preferring my own interest before obedience to the Church and the pleasure of my God? To fast in order to save is good, to fast in order to obey the Church is better, to fast in order to please God is best: but though it may seem that with three goods one cannot make a bad; yet he who should place them out of order, preferring the less to the better, would without doubt commit an irregularity deserving of blame. (*Treatise on the Love of God*)

Discern Always

We hope we've communicated the importance of fasting as a Christian. Although we don't support the idea that fasting is a positive health trend, this in no way negates our religious obligations. There are times, though, when strict fasts from food may not be prudent, and should be discussed with a trusted priest or spiritual director. The Church already outlines some of these guidelines for us (pregnant/nursing mothers, young children, elderly), but there may be additional seasons of life when serious fasting could do more harm.

St. Jerome writes, "He who immoderately afflicts his body either by eating too little food, or by taking too little sleep, offers a sacrifice of theft." What does he mean by "sacrifice of theft"? If the way in which we are fasting seriously hinders us in fulfilling our duties to those entrusted to us (spouse, children, work, ministry, etc.), we may need to discern if the way we are fasting is appropriate. St. Francis de Sales furthers this idea by saying, "A want of moderation in the use of fasting, discipline and austerity has made many a one useless in works of charity during the best years of his life."

These gray areas are for personal discernment, with a trusted spiritual advisor whenever possible. We need to be honest with ourselves about our state in life, our capacity, as well as our weaknesses and desire for comfort. And when it seems clear that God is not asking us to restrict general nourishment, how can we deny ourselves in other meaningful ways? May we pray for rightly-ordered hearts and minds as we enter into the season of Lent, a time where we ought to experience time in the desert with Jesus.

"Can it be that Christ's passion alone was insufficient to save us? No.
It left nothing more to be done; it was more than sufficient to save all men.
However, for the merits of the Passion to be applied to us, according to
St. Thomas Aquinas, we need to cooperate (subjective redemption) by patiently
bearing the trials God sends us, so as to become like our head, Christ."

—St. Alphonsus Ligouri

Tending the Garden as a Prayer

"Therefore we are to see a certain vision, my brethren, that no eye has seen, nor ear heard, nor the heart of man conceived: a vision surpassing all earthly beauty, whether it be that of gold and silver, woods and fields, sea and sky, sun and moon, or stars and angels. The reason is this: it is the source of all other beauty."

— St. Augustine

In November of 2009, Pope Benedict XVI had a meeting in the Sistine Chapel with a few hundred artists. He addressed them as "custodians" or "guardians" of beauty and shared many profound remarks on the importance of beauty as people of faith. He said, "Authentic beauty ... unlocks the yearning of the human heart, the profound desire to know, to love, to go towards the Other, to reach for the Beyond. If we acknowledge that beauty touches us intimately, that it wounds us, that it opens our eyes, then we rediscover the joy of seeing, of being able to grasp the profound meaning of our existence, the Mystery of which we are part; from this Mystery we can draw fullness, happiness, the passion to engage with it every day." The late pope also quoted St. Paul VI when he said, "This world in which we live needs beauty in order not to sink into despair. Beauty, like truth, brings joy to the human heart, and is that precious fruit which resists the erosion of time, which unites generations and enables them to be one in admiration. And all this through the work of your hands . . . Remember that you are the guardians of beauty in the world."

Not many of us truly consider ourselves artists. We go about life, accomplishing tasks, wiping counters, hugging friends, kissing little cheeks. But it is a beautiful thing to ponder — the admiration of the Lord's creation as a profound prayer, as well as the small ways we can create beauty in our homes as gifts for those around us. How can we be more intentional with this? One of the things so many of us long for with the return of spring: to be back in the garden. To tend, to nurture, to admire, to get our hands in the soil and create something out of a seemingly plain spot, however small or large. The separation from nature that often coincides with the bitterly cold days of late winter often causes an even deeper longing for the warm sunshine and new growth that seem so very far away. To everything there is a season, and the return of spring with its lushness, color, and light is truly a beautiful tiny glimpse into the Creator's eternity.

"Creation is the beginning and the foundation of all God's works."

— CCC 198

Potager Gardens

What are potager gardens and what do they have to do with our prayer? Potager, pronounced "pow-tuh-jay," literally translated from French means, "for the soup pot." A potager garden is essentially a kitchen garden with both practical and aesthetic value. Their history actually stretches all the way back to the monasteries of Medieval times. As Jennifer Bartley notes in *Designing the New Kitchen Garden: An American Potager Handbook*,

> The term potager carries with it a much deeper historical tradition. This meaning stretched back to the Middle Ages when all of Western civilization — literature, history, science — was hanging by a slender thread, hidden behind the high stone walls of medieval monasteries. These cultural outposts were small, isolated, and largely self-sufficient. For the most part, monks and nuns grew their own food, herbs, and medicines. Within small geometric plots, useful herbs, vegetables, and perhaps some flowers were grown for daily use. Monastery gardens were more than vegetable gardens, however; they were also used as sites for meditation and prayer.

You may consider yourself a seasoned gardener or just a novice, but gardening has something to teach all of us. The question is, how can we take this idea of the potager, a place of beauty, color, life, and practicality, and apply it to our own homes and gardens? To create spaces, however large or small, that turn our gazes upward and make us pause and admire the beauty? Garden writer Joy Larkcom said, "Potagers are like painting pictures in your garden: the colors of the vegetables, flowers and herbs are your palette."

7 Tips for Creating Your Potager:

1. Incorporate plenty of variety into your space.

Herbs can be planted among flowers which can be scattered among the veggies. Potager gardens are known for being practical spaces, often right outside the kitchen door, where you grow the things you eat and enjoy. So don't be afraid to mix some new things in with old tried-and-true favorites, like a handful of lovely new-found varieties.

2. Grow things that you know you and your family will eat and enjoy.

If you don't love tomatoes, don't feel like you have to grow them just because you are a home gardener. If you prefer bouquets with softer colors, keep this in mind when picking out flower varieties.

3. Add texture.

Plants like globe thistles, dahlias, lamb's ear, lupines, zinnias, and even curly kale and cabbage can add more interest with their various textures.

4. Use succession planting.

Once a crop finishes out, like early-planted potatoes, greens, carrots, etc., plan to fill that space in the garden again to have things growing all season. Also, if an annual flops, falls victim to pests, or doesn't sprout, try not to get discouraged and just sow a few more seeds.

5. Mix perennials with annuals.

It's good for adding depth to the garden to continue to tend to returning perennials, and it's good for the soil too! You can plan each year to fill gaps between the perennial plants with annual ones.

6. Use height.

Arbors and trellises are a lovely way to do this, where you can grow things like sweet peas, beans, cucumbers, small pumpkins, climbing roses, morning glory, clematis, etc. This can be as simple as tying together some bamboo poles, or you can get fancy with a DIY project.

7. Tend to the health of the soil.

Continue to work to enhance the life underground by applying good quality compost yearly, mulching with organic materials, limiting your disturbance of the soil, and avoiding the use of harsh chemicals.

Celebrating St. Joseph

by Maria Fredriksson

March 19th is the solemnity of St. Joseph, husband of Mary. While cultures across the world have their own customs and traditions for this great feast, which always falls in the midst of Lent, there are notable ones that go especially far back in devotion to the saint.

The region of Sicilia in Italy has some of the longest lasting traditions honoring St. Joseph. The day is traditionally filled with feasting, but with meatless food. During the Middle Ages, Sicilia was struggling with famine due to a severe drought. They promised God that if He answered their prayers through the intercession of St. Joseph and brought them rain they would prepare a feast in honor of the saint. Rain came to them, saving their fava bean crop, and forever after March 19th has been a *festa* for the Foster father of the Savior. This gave rise to the traditional *Maccu di San Giuseppe* dish also known as Fava Beans because that was the food that saved the Sicilians from starvation.

It is also customary to eat on St. Joseph's Day a famous baked or deep-fried pastry stuffed with cream and topped with candied fruit known as *Sfinge* in Sicilia and sometimes *Zeppole* in Napoli and Eastern Italy. Other special foods on the day usually include Minestrone (a vegetable soup) or *Pasta di San Giuseppe,* which was a unique pasta dish made with bread crumbs to symbolize the sawdust from St. Joseph's carpentry work. The foods are usually displayed on a special altar called "St. Joseph's Table" or "La Tavola di San Giuseppe," which is always blessed by the priest.

Another popular custom in Italy that is related to the table and feast is "Tupa Tupa." It means "Knock Knock" and entails a reenactment where three children dressed as the Holy Family knock on three doors asking for shelter. The first two doors turn them away (in memory of the Holy Family at the inns in Bethlehem), but at the third door they are finally welcomed with the shout "Viva la tavola di San Giuseppe!" after which the feasting begins. This custom is not as well known as the St. Joseph Altar, but it is particularly touching as a remembrance of St. Joseph since he was the one who had the most heartache over the lack of shelter as he was the protector and provider of Our Lady and the Holy Child.

The final main component of St. Joseph's Day observed across Italy is the wearing of red. Not only is it a vivid color of celebration — which the medieval mind must have loved — but red is also one of Italy's national colors.

Minestrone

for St. Joseph's Day (March 19)

by Maria Fredriksson

Yields 10 servings.

Ingredients:

- 4 Tbsp olive oil
- 6 cloves garlic, chopped
- 2 onions, chopped
- 1 cup celery, chopped
- 5 carrots, sliced
- 6 cups vegetable stock (use tomato sauce or water if extra liquid is needed)
- Large can diced tomatoes in juice
- Large can crushed tomatoes in juice
- Large jar Great Northern or Cannellini beans
- 2 small zucchini, quartered and sliced
- 2 summer squash, quartered and sliced
- 1 1/2 cups fresh or frozen corn kernels (or 1 16 oz can of corn)
- 1 1/2 lbs fresh spinach, torn (or 1 pkg. frozen, chopped spinach)
- 2 Tbsp chopped fresh oregano (or 2 tsp dried)
- 1 Tbsp chopped fresh basil (or 1 tsp dried)
- 2 Tbsp chopped fresh thyme (or 2 tsp dried)
- 1 Tbsp fennel seeds
- Salt and pepper, to taste

Instructions:

1. Over medium-low heat, in a large pot heat olive oil and sauté garlic for 2 to 3 minutes. Do not let it brown.

2. Add onion and sauté for 4 to 5 minutes. Add celery and carrots, sauté for 1 to 2 minutes more. Add stock and bring to a boil, stirring frequently.

3. Reduce to low heat and add beans, corn, spinach, zucchini, squash, oregano, basil, fennel seeds, salt and pepper. Simmer an hour.

4. Ladle soup into bowls and add cooked pasta if desired. Sprinkle cheeses on top. Drizzle with olive oil and serve with crusty bread. Traditionally, minestrone is thought to be better the next day.

For topping:

- Small pasta, cooked separately just before serving *(optional)*
- Shredded provolone and grated parmesan
- 1 Tbsp olive oil

Sfinge or Zeppole di San Giuseppe

for St. Joseph's Day (March 19)

by Maria Fredriksson

Yields 12-20 pastries.

For the dough:

- 1 cup water

- 1/3 cup unsalted butter

- 1 Tbsp sugar

- Grated rind of 1 lemon

- Pinch of salt

- 1 cup sifted flour

- 4 large eggs at room temperature

- 1 Tbsp vanilla

For the filling:

- 2 cups ricotta cheese

- 1/2 cup confectioners' sugar

- 1/2 tsp vanilla

- 1/4 tsp ground cinnamon

- 1/3 cup grated dark chocolate (optional)

- 2 Tbsp finely chopped pistachios (optional)

For the garnish:

- Powdered sugar

- Candied fruit or maraschino cherries

Instructions:

1. Put water, butter, granulated sugar, lemon rind, and salt in a large saucepan. Bring to a boil, and as soon as the butter has melted, remove from heat. Add the flour all at once, stirring constantly and with vigor.

2. Return the pan to the heat, and stir constantly until the mixture forms a ball and comes away from the sides of the pan. Cook just a little longer, until you hear a slight crackling, frying sound.

3. Remove the pan from the heat and cool slightly. Add the eggs, one at a time. Be sure that each egg is thoroughly blended into the mixture before you add the next. Stir until smooth and thoroughly blended. Add the vanilla. Cover the dough and let it stand for 15 to 20 minutes.

4. Preheat the oven to 400 degrees F. If you would prefer to deep fry in lard the way zeppole is usually made, heat your lard and pipe the dough into large circles on pieces of parchment paper so that you can drop it into the lard for deep frying.

5. Drop the dough by heaping tablespoons on a buttered cookie sheet or onto a parchment-lined baking sheet, leaving 2 inches between the sfinge. Bake for 20 to 25 minutes, until golden brown. Remove from oven and cool.

6. Mix the ricotta, confectioners' sugar, vanilla, cinnamon, chocolate, and pistachios. Just before serving, cut off the tops of the sfinge and fill; place top back on after filling. Arrange on a platter, sprinkle with powdered sugar, and garnish each pastry with a candied fruit.

Dynamic Celebrations

by Eryn Goldstein

Celebrations are a wonderful and life-giving aspect of the human experience. Throughout each year, gathering with friends and family to commemorate milestones and important dates can enliven days filled with ordinary tasks and routines. Modern celebrations are full of joy and meaningful traditions, but often also include large bouts of sedentary time, which can leave our bodies lacking the movement they need for true wellbeing. This is especially true at times of year when the weather makes indoor gatherings more comfortable and convenient. Luckily, we don't have to choose between nourishing our souls and our bodies, as I have been reminded through the writing of biomechanist Katy Bowman. Katy uses the term "dynamic celebrations" to describe gatherings that intentionally include a variety of movement and connection to nature. Katy's approach suggests that, rather than taking good things out of our celebrations, we focus on making our special times even better by infusing them with movement, nature, and community.

Dynamic celebrations come naturally to us as Catholics. We have a treasure of dynamic traditions within the historical celebrations of the Church. Many of the long-standing customs for observing the liturgical year are connected to the changing of seasons, the labor and bounty of growing and harvesting food, and worshiping God through prayer that requires movement and physical effort. There are many established Catholic traditions that can be rediscovered and adopted to incorporate more movement and nature into our celebrations. Yet, a simple and wonderful way to begin is to consider how your own favorite customs can be adapted to include more movement and outdoor fun. This could be as easy as moving your festivities outdoors to eat sitting on the lawn, or sourcing your party decorations from natural sources. Start with something that is inspiring and joyful for you!

General Ideas to Consider When Planning a Celebration

- Plan time to walk to get food for special meals. This could mean walking to a grocery store or local farm, or foraging for wild berries, greens, or apples.

- Eat outside! Setting up a table or picnic area for a special meal can be a wonderful way to enjoy the outdoors while sharing in community. Or, take a seasonal drink or dessert with you on a walk after your meal.

- Grow or gather food items and decorations. Invite friends and family to join you for a foraging hike to collect items for wreaths, bouquets, or other seasonal decorations.

- Plan ahead to grow some of your own food or flowers for your favorite meals and gatherings throughout the year. Tending to a few special crops offers a deeper connection to traditional foods and décor and can add to the joy of anticipating a celebration!

LENT

Prayer

- Invite friends and family to pray the Stations of the Cross outdoors. Find an outdoor trail with stations, or create your own.

- Take a walk each day to pray a Rosary or meditate on Scripture.

- Plan a weekly meet-up with friends for prayer and a simple soup dinner outdoors. This could be at someone's home or a local park.

Fasting

- Walk instead of driving or taking public transportation to church, the grocery store, work/school, or another place that you go frequently.

- Avoid using your most comfortable furniture, or try sitting on the floor with bolsters to support your body. This could be all of the time, or just for prayer or meals.

- Write a handwritten letter to connect with a friend or family member instead of texting or emailing for non-urgent communication.

Almsgiving

- Find opportunities to serve those who cannot move easily. Offer to help neighbors, family members, or fellow parishioners with spring yard work or housecleaning.

- Volunteer to prepare or serve a meal at a community kitchen or help sort and pack food at a food bank.

- Reach out to local farms to ask if they donate produce to charities. If you find one that does, volunteer to help with harvest or delivery.

EASTER

- Give suggestions for setting up an outdoor/dynamic seating area for an Easter meal or gathering. I think it would be fun to show that it can look festive/"normal" to set a low table that allows for floor seating. You could show ways of including different types of seating for people who have varied movement limitations or bolstering needs.

- Offer tips for foraging spring branches/decorations for Easter.

- Host a dessert walk or hike during the Easter season.

- Plan a bonfire gathering or decorate your house with flowers for Pentecost.

Waffles

for Our Lady's Day, the Solemnity of the Annunciation (March 25)

by Marisa Fredrickson

In Swedish, the word for Our Lady's Day is Vårfrudagen. When said quickly, the word Vårfrudagen sounds close to våffeldagen (waffle). Because of this, it has become a Swedish tradition to eat waffles on the Feast of the Annunciation.

Ingredients:

- 2 cups flour *(substitute gluten free if needed)*

- 1 tsp baking powder

- 1/2 tsp baking soda

- 6 Tbsp salted butter, melted

- 4 eggs

- 1 cup milk

Instructions:

1. Preheat your waffle iron.

2. Whisk together flour, baking powder, and baking soda.

3. In a separate bowl, whisk the eggs, milk, yogurt, and melted butter.

4. Pour the wet ingredients into the dry, and gently whisk to combine. Don't worry if it seems lumpy.

5. Brush your waffle iron with butter or coconut oil, and cook the waffles according to your iron's directions. Serve immediately.

6. Leftover waffles can be stored on the counter for 2 days, or frozen for 2 months. Simply pop them in the toaster to reheat.

Hot Cross Buns

for Good Friday
by Genie Shaw

As the Holy Week cousin of Hallowtide soul cakes, hot cross buns are essentially yeasted rolls seasoned with aromatic spices and a mix of dried fruit. Traditionally they are eaten on Good Friday as a small collation for that required day of fasting and abstinence. It was customary for ancient Christians to bless fresh loaves of bread with the sign of the cross and this practice has continued for hundreds of years. Going back to the middle of the 1300s, at the English Abbey of St. Alban's the monks gave hot cross buns to the poor as a form of almsgiving on Good Friday. This is a beautiful tradition that we can continue in our time by taking hot cross buns to friends, donating to local food banks, or taking food donations to nearby monastic houses that rely on our charity for survival.

Ingredients:

- 4 1/2 cups flour
- 1/4 cup light brown sugar
- 1 Tbsp baking powder
- 1/2 tsp nutmeg
- 1/2 tsp cloves
- 2 tsp cinnamon
- 1 3/4 tsp salt
- Zest of an orange
- 6 Tbsp softened butter
- 1 1/4 cups room-temperature milk
- 2 tsp instant yeast
- 3 large eggs, divided
- 1/4 cup rum or fruit juice like orange
- 1 cup dried fruit of your choice

For the Easter icing crosses:

- 1 cup & 2 Tbsp powdered sugar
- Sprinkle of salt
- 1/2 tsp vanilla extract
- Up to 4 teaspoons milk

Instructions:

1. Combine the dried fruit and your choice of rum or juice in a small bowl, then heat until warm. Set it aside. In a large bowl incorporate all the remaining ingredients but the one separated egg white. Next knead the dough until it becomes soft and elastic. It is super sticky at first. Now add in the dried fruit mixture, liquid and all.

2. Cover the dough and allow it to rise for about an hour. Meanwhile, butter a 9x13-inch pan, then divide the dough into golfball-sized pieces and shape them into balls. Place the dough balls in your buttered pan, cover, and let rise for another hour or so.

3. About halfway through this rise, preheat your oven to 375 degrees. To make the paste for your crosses, mix flour and water to the consistency of pancake mix. Pour the mixture into a ziplock bag and cut off one small corner to make a piping bag. A thicker mix makes it easier to work with since it won't run as much.

4. After the buns are finished rising, whisk up the remaining egg white with a tiny splash of milk. Brush the tops of the buns with it, then add your paste crosses. Finally, bake the buns for at least 20 minutes or until golden brown.

Rosary Reflections for Spring

by Emily Patteson

As the frost melts, the days get brighter, and the world gets greener, it can be easy to want the warmth to arrive as fast as possible. As we embrace the spring's transitional weather and bask in the glory of Easter, let us reflect on this fourth set of Rosary mysteries. The glorious mysteries unite us to Jesus' victory, Mary's journey alongside Jesus, and the anticipation of the changing season. Through this time as we prepare for and celebrate Easter, we seek to unite ourselves to God through time spent with Mary.

Opening prayer: Lord, as the frost melts outside, please melt my heart. Make it soft and ready to accept all that You want me to hear during this time. May I be united to the growth and expectation of this earthly season, and may it illuminate all that You are doing in my heart in this season of my life. I am open and ready to be united to You in this time of prayer. Amen.

The Resurrection

"Then the angel said to the women in reply, 'Do not be afraid! I know that you are seeking Jesus the crucified. He is not here, for he has been raised just as he said. Come and see the place where he lay. Then go quickly and tell his disciples, "He has been raised from the dead, and he is going before you to Galilee; there you will see him." Behold, I have told you.'" (Matthew 28:5-7)

Christ, You rose from the dead, and this gives us hope for new life! St. Vincent Ferrer preached: "But the greatest of all [feast days] is Easter Day, the day of the Lord's Resurrection, because today assurance was given to us to obtain eternal and immortal life in soul and body. Christ gave it to us through his resurrection, which is the cause and the assurance of our resurrection." *Rejoice in this promise of renewal and healing.*

The women find out about Jesus' rising from the angel, and then they bring the message to the disciples. The Lord's Resurrection was a relatively silent and hidden event. In the same way, we reflect on the silence of the new life of growing flowers and other plants. This shows us that we must look in the silent and hidden places of our own hearts for healing and renewal. *How might your desire for visible life-altering renewal keep you from recognizing the little ways God is growing you?*

The Ascension of Jesus into Heaven

"May the God of hope fill you with all joy and peace in believing, so that you may abound in hope by the power of the holy Spirit." (Romans 15:13)

Jesus Christ, You rose to Heaven and go before us to be united to God the Father. You won victory over death by dying and rising, and by this we hope to be united with You again. As St. John Paul II has exhorted us; "I plead with you — never, ever give up on hope; never doubt, never tire, and never become discouraged. Be not afraid." *Lord, may Your ascending into Heaven always be a sign of hope and expectation for me.*

This mystery is one of anticipation and expectation because of what Jesus did for us and where a life lived following Him will lead us. Let this be what drives us to live out our faith, especially when it isn't easy. This is similar to planting a garden in the spring. We hoe, dig, plant, and water. All that work leaves the ground looking more or less the same. However, we do all of this driven by the anticipation of what it will eventually look like. *Reflect on what Jesus' rising and ascending into Heaven means for you. How can you let this change the way you live your life today?*

The Descent of the Holy Spirit

"And I will ask the Father, and he will give you another Advocate to be with you always, the Spirit of truth, which the world cannot accept, because it neither sees nor knows it. But you know it, because it remains with you, and will be in you." (John 14:16-17)

Jesus, You returned to Your Father in Heaven, but You did not leave us alone. You gave us the gift of the Holy Spirit to be with us always. Just as St. Mary Magdalen de Pazzi wrote: "Spirit of truth, you are the reward of the saints, the comforter of souls, light in the darkness, riches to the poor, treasure to lovers, food for the hungry, comfort to those who are wandering; to sum up, you are the one in whom all treasures are contained." *God, thank You for the gift of Your Holy Spirit dwelling among us.*

How beautiful it is that the God of love cares for us, and, in His endless love, gave us an advocate. The Spirit should be the one upon which we rely to lead and guide us. We must let go of self-reliance, any thoughts of being able to do anything on our own. Reflect on all the magnificent roles of the Holy Spirit and seek to let it be all of them for you. *In what ways do I rely on my own self rather than on the Advocate? Resolve to make one deliberate act of reliance on the Holy Spirit this week.*

The Assumption of Mary into Heaven

"Mary said, 'Behold, I am the handmaid of the Lord. May it be done to me according to your word.'" (Luke 1:38)

Mary, on Earth you were perfectly united to God's will and when you died you were united with God in Heaven. St. Alphonsus Ligouri reminds us in his *Uniformity with God's Will* that "Mary was the most perfect among the saints only because she was always perfectly united to the will of God." *Lord, I desire to be united to Your will and join You and Our Lady in Heaven when I die.*

When we unite ourselves to the will of God, we worship God and act perfectly in accordance with our own nature. The sun shines, trees blow in the wind, seedlings sprout. All of these things made by God always act in accordance with how they were created. When they do so, they glorify their Creator. *What is one area of your life in which you fail to unite yourself to God's will for you or even act without asking what His will is? God, help me to be like the created world around me and glorify You.*

Mary Is Crowned as the Queen of Heaven

"A great sign appeared in the sky, a woman clothed with the sun, with the moon under her feet, and on her head a crown of twelve stars." (Revelation 12:1)

Mary, you were made Queen of Heaven by God, and we thank you for interceding for us. Pope Pius IX teaches us that, "With a heart that is truly a mother's ... does she approach the problem of our salvation, and is solicitous for the whole human race. ... She intercedes powerfully for us with a mother's prayers, obtains what she seeks, and cannot be refused." (*Ad Caeli Reginam*, 42). *Help us to rely more readily on Mary's motherly intercession.*

As women, we have been given the gift of the feminine genius and the call to mother others on our paths, both physically and spiritually. Relying on Mary's intercession looks like turning to her intercession for our prayers. It also involves following her example when God calls us to mother others. Further, we must humbly accept our own need for mothering and allow Mary to love us in our own need. *If one of these areas sticks out to you, ask the Lord how you can let Mary be your mother and Queen of your heart in that way.*

Closing prayer: Lord, I thank You for this time in prayer. Help me to grow in hope as I anticipate all that You are doing in my life. I seek to rely on both the Holy Spirit and Mary, gifts You have given to lead me to You. May I go forth from this time changed by the ways that You have moved. I hold onto the joy of this season knowing that You have conquered death and can conquer anything else I struggle with. Amen.

Natural Easter Egg Dyes

for Easter

by Maria Fredriksson

Enjoy the simplicity of making Easter eggs with natural dyes. You can use white or brown eggs; brown eggs, in fact, dye a richer color with natural dyes.

The same process applies to each of the natural dyes listed:

1. Rinse and chop the food item. Bring 2 quarts of water to boil. Add the food item and simmer until the color of the water reaches the darkness of color you desire.

2. Strain the colored water (your dye) into a tall bowl or wide-mouth glass mason jar. The taller the bowl the better, as you want to cover the eggs. Compost the food pieces. Let the dye cool. (You can add 1 teaspoon of white vinegar to each jar when ready to dye the eggs, as it helps the color to leech into the egg shell. Be aware that adding vinegar and baking soda to the cabbage dye is what turns it from purple to a teal blue. If you are intending to draw designs with your white wax or crayon, now is the time to do so.)

3. Lower your eggs into the jars or bowls with a slotted spoon. Leave the eggs in the dye until they reach the depth of color you would like. Remember that natural dyes take much longer to color an egg. This is where a wide-mouth quart mason jar is helpful because you can fit multiple eggs in at once. Place back in the egg carton or in an egg holder to dry. Store them in the refrigerator.

Tips: make sure your eggs are completely cool before dyeing them. Hard boiling them the day before and refrigerating overnight seems to work best. If you would like the deepest colors you can get, plan to leave your eggs in the dye on a shelf in the refrigerator overnight.

Light or Magenta Pink - Beets
Use 3 beets (peeled and chopped) per 4 cups of water. Boil for 15 to 30 minutes.

Purple - Red/Purple Cabbage
Use ½ cup chopped cabbage (remove outer leaves and chop) per 1 cup of water. Boil for 15 minutes.

Teal Blue - Red/Purple Cabbage with Baking Soda
Repeat mixture for purple; once the mixture is cooled and the vinegar mixed in, add about 1/2 teaspoon of baking soda.

Pale, Pearly Gray-Blue - Blueberries
Boil for 15 minutes, then strain.

Light, Golden Yellow - Yellow Onion Skins
Use skins from 3 onions per 4 cups of water. Boil for 15 minutes.

Bright Golden Yellow - Turmeric
Add 1 Tbsp of turmeric per 4 cups of water. Boil for 15 minutes.

THE TRADITIONAL EASTER BASKET

by Maria Fredriksson

The tradition of the Easter Basket can be traced back as far as the 1200s. There are many variations, but we are drawing from Eastern European customs. The traditional Easter basket is tied to both the Lenten Fast as well as the customary food blessing in older Rites on Holy Saturday. You can find the traditional blessings in the *Rituale Romanum.* The blessing typically takes place in the morning of Easter Saturday when people bring their food in linen covered baskets often decorated with greenery. When the contents of the basket are being used for the breakfasts of Easter Sunday, Monday, and Tuesday, they usually contain everything from early spring greens to multiple types of sweet breads and cakes to soft cheese, butter, sausage, ham, and horseradish. To make your own traditional Easter basket (you can make small versions to give to friends!), use the following seven traditional items:

1. White linen - often richly embroidered and passed down in families, the white linen both lines the basket and goes over the food as a covering.

2. A wicker basket - any sturdy woven basket with a strong, stiff handle will work.

3. A white or beeswax candle - a candle, often tied with a red ribbon, is included in the basket to be lit during the blessing. It represents Christ as the Light of the World. On Holy Saturday, when the tabernacle is starkly open and the altar bare and no light has been lit since Tenebrae, the candles during the food blessing are just one more quiet anticipation of the Vigil to come.

4. Butter Lamb - butter or dairy is one of the main foods originally given up in the Great Lent fast of the ancient Church. Thus, the custom of making a butter lamb to bring to church for the blessing is often an integral part of the traditional basket. Its twofold symbolism includes the joy of the Easter feast as well as the more obvious representation of the Lamb of God.

5. Salt - often given up during the Lenten Fast, salt is added in to bring zest to life and preserve us from corruption.

6. Pisanki (Hardboiled Eggs) - authentic *pisanki* are the most well-known Easter eggs with their intricate designs drawn in beeswax and multiple colors of dye. But authentic or not, the eggs are indicative of new life and the Resurrection. Early Church traditions included people walking around with Easter eggs dyed brilliant red on Easter Sunday and knocking them together in greeting with other people to symbolize the stone being rolled from the tomb.

7. Sweet Bread - the glorious point of *Paska* is that it includes all the rich foods given up during the Lenten fast — eggs, milk, butter, salt, yeast, and honey or sugar. If the *Paska* is too big to fit in the basket, it is often wrapped in its own white linen cloth.

Other items that may be included are: **kolbasa** (sausage), which symbolizes the chains of death broken when Jesus rose from the dead and God's generosity in doing so; **bacon,** which symbolizes the abundance of God's mercy; **horseradish**, a reminder of the bitterness and harshness of the Passion of Jesus, and the vinegar it is mixed with to symbolize the sour wine given to Jesus on the Cross; **ham** or **lamb** to symbolize great joy and abundance in the celebration of Christ's Resurrection; and **hrudka** (a soft, sweet cheese), a reminder to be moderate in feasting.

How to Make a Butter Lamb

Acquire a pound of butter in one block or four sticks. Set it out on the counter to warm up until it is fairly malleable. The butter will get more malleable as you work with it. Make sure you have clean hands and expect to get them very buttery before you are done. Wax paper on your workspace makes a good surface for working on. If you have four sticks of butter, put two lengthwise together and the third stick in the middle on top of them. Use one half of the fourth stick to make a neck and face for your lamb and smooth it onto the "body." Once the neck and head are smoothed on, stick a toothpick through the neck and into the main body to add extra reinforcement. You can smooth over where the toothpick went in so that no one knows the difference. Use the other half of the fourth stick to add ears, to round out the sides and bum of the lamb, and to add a little tail. Details such as wool texture and eyes can be added by shaping with a butter or frosting knife. Cut the wax paper to size and put in a bread pan or other larger container. It hardens best if kept in the freezer for a few hours, but the refrigerator overnight also works well. When gifting a basket to others after the Easter Vigil, you can wrap it in plastic to keep it frozen until the last moment. If you want a much larger butter lamb, use more butter sticks accordingly or use two large butter rolls of a pound each to piece the lamb together.

You may add a Paschal Banner. Cut out the shape of the flag in paper, color on the red cross, attach to a skewer or toothpick, and poke into the lamb at an angle over its shoulder.

Paska Recipe

The recipe below is a Polish version of *Paska* bread. There are two main ways of shaping it. One is to put the dough in a tall rounded cylinder such as an old coffee container or aluminum can with the tops cut off. The other way is to braid the dough into a very thick, tall circle. Sometimes bakers will use a rounded tin to put the bulk of the dough in and then decorate it with a large braid on top.

Bread ingredients:

- 5 cups all-purpose flour
- 2 1/4 tsp (1 packet) instant dry yeast
- 1/4 cup granulated sugar or substitute honey
- 2 1/2 tsp salt
- 1 cup lukewarm water
- 1/2 cup whole milk
- 2 large eggs
- 1/4 cup (4 Tbsp) unsalted butter, at room temperature

Topping:

- 1 large egg
- 1 Tbsp water
- 1 Tbsp granulated sugar

Instructions:

1. Using a stand mixer or wooden spoon, mix and knead all of the dough ingredients — flour through butter — until it comes together into a soft, smooth ball. The dough should be pliable, not very sticky, and bounce back when poked lightly with your finger. Place the dough in a lightly greased bowl and set aside on the counter. Allow it to rise for 60-90 minutes, until nearly doubled in size. Meanwhile, lightly grease a 9-inch round pan and set aside. (I love using a springform pan for this, but a cake pan also works well.)

2. Turn the dough out onto a lightly floured work surface. Pull off about a quarter of it — you'll use this to form the braids. Shape the remaining large piece of dough into a smooth ball, and place in the center of the prepared pan. Divide the reserved piece of dough into three equal pieces, and roll each one out into a strand about 18-20 inches. Use these three strands to create one long braid.

3. Cut the braid in half, then place in a cross on top of the larger piece of dough in the pan. (Alternatively, you could wrap the braid in one length around the inside edge of the pan.) Cover the loaf and let rise for about 45 minutes, until approximately doubled in size. Near the end of the rising time, preheat the oven to 350 degrees and place a rack in the lower-middle.

4. When the bread has risen, make the topping. Beat the egg and water together with a fork in a small bowl, and brush the mixture gently over the loaf. Sprinkle with additional sugar, as desired.

5. Bake bread for 35 to 45 minutes, until the top is a rich golden brown. Remove from the oven and let cool completely before cutting and serving.

To Begin Anew

by Susanna Parent

Years after his Easter Vigil homily, I am still thinking about Pope Francis' evergreen message. As our shepherd, he gently and beautifully shares three main points.

1. It Is Always Possible to Begin Anew

After Jesus' death on the Cross, "Mary Magdalene, Mary, the mother of James, and Salome brought spices so that they might go and anoint him" (Mark 16:1). They finally reached His tomb, just as the sun was rising. Scripture says they were "utterly amazed" when they saw an angel near the tomb instead of a guard. But the angel said to spread the word that Jesus was *going before them* to Galilee, and it is there that they would find Him. In Pope Francis' words, "To go to Galilee means, first, *to begin anew*." Isn't it interesting that this beginning anew actually required going back to where Jesus first called them to Himself? "The place of their first encounter and the place of their first love." How often do I long for a fresh start and a forgetting of a tainted past. But that's not what Jesus is asking. He's asking us to begin again by *going back* to the place where we found Him, and oftentimes that is in places of darkness and suffering. The Lord isn't limited or intimidated by our weaknesses and faults. He sees beyond. He sees our potential. He desires to create new life in us and birth a new spirit of hope in our hearts. "Let us go to Galilee, then, to discover that God cannot be filed away among our childhood memories, but is alive and filled with surprises. Risen from the dead, Jesus never ceases to amaze us." Just like He amazed the women who saw the angel at the tomb.

"For see, the winter is past,
the rains are over and gone.
The flowers appear on the earth,
the time of pruning the vines has come,
and the song of the turtledove is heard in our land.
The fig tree puts forth its figs,
and the vines, in bloom, give forth fragrance.
Arise, my friend, my beautiful one, and come!"

— Song of Songs 2:11-13

2. Jesus Is Alive Here and Now

What Pope Francis wants us to know here, is that Jesus is with us in every moment of every day. Trials. Hopes. Dreams. Jesus "urges you not to indulge in nostalgia for the past or cynicism about the present." Again, Jesus wants to surprise you. As my three-year-old daughter would say, "keep your eyes peeled" and watch for the ways big and small, that the Holy Spirit is working in your life. It might be small. It might just be the soft radiance of a rainbow on a dark day or, for my mom, seeing a cardinal. What I know for sure is that the Holy Spirit is alive and well and, if we are asking and watching, He will surely make Himself known, because He wants to delight you and show you that He sees you and He hears you.

When Jesus went to Galilee, He was going to the peripheries. He began His mission in the place where He knew He would find the impoverished and the vulnerable, those who were discouraged and those who were lost. Pope Francis speaks about how Jesus is asking us to go "to the real 'Galilee' of our daily life. … There the Lord goes ahead of us and makes Himself present in the lives of those around us, those who share in our day, our home, our work, our difficulties and hopes." Here we find Christ's face. "We will be amazed how the greatness of God is revealed in littleness, how his beauty shines forth in the poor and simple."

3. Jesus Loves Us Without Limits

Finally, the pope's third message: Jesus' love for us is limitless and His presence is undoubtable. When we are able to overcome our judgements and grudges, we "rediscover the *grace of everyday life.*" As a woman who knows how to hold a good grudge (and the pain it only brings to myself), I could use some of this grace in my life! Here is where I need to heed the words of our Holy Father and open my heart to the amazement of the Easter message. As the angel said to the women at the tomb, "Do not be afraid! He has been raised just as he said" (Matthew 28:5-6). Just a few verses later we see that Jesus meets them on their way. He anticipates their arrival.

He anticipates our arrival too. Flaws and all. But He also calls us on. He wants to challenge us to begin anew. To say no to the hot breath of Satan's whispers in our ears. And we can do it, because we've got the help of the Holy Spirit and Jesus Himself walking alongside us. To close with the reminder of Pope Francis, "the Lord always goes ahead of you, he always walks before you. And, with him, life always begins anew."

Carrot Cake

for Easter

by Marisa Fredrickson

Ingredients:

- 2 1/2 sticks salted butter
- 6 eggs
- 1 cup cane sugar
- 2/3 cup packed brown sugar or coconut sugar
- 1 tsp vanilla extract
- 2 1/2 cups all-purpose flour*
- 4 tsp baking powder
- 3 tsp baking soda
- 2 tsp cinnamon
- 3 1/2 cups peeled and grated carrots
- 1 1/3 cup puréed canned peaches (strain the juice first) or applesauce

to make gluten free, substitute 2 cups gluten-free flour plus 1/2 cup almond flour. The almond flour is optional, though it creates an amazing texture in gluten-free cakes.

Instructions:

1. Preheat oven to 350 degrees. Melt the butter over the stove, and meanwhile in a bowl or stand mixer, whisk together eggs and sugars until the sugar dissolves and the mixture becomes fluffy. Slowly pour in the melted butter and whisk thoroughly. In a separate bowl, combine your flour, cinnamon, baking powder, and soda. Whisk flour mixture into your batter, then add grated carrot along with the peach purée or applesauce, and stir just until combined.

2. Prep your cake pans by tracing them on parchment paper and cutting out the rounds. Grease your pans with coconut oil, then place the rounds in the bottom. This will help your cakes to come out beautifully.

3. Divide batter evenly among 3 6" cake pans or 2 8" pans. Bake about 40 minutes, or just until a toothpick comes out clean. The tops may look a little brown, but this is normal. Run a knife along the pan edges before turning the cakes out, allow to cool, then wrap in cling film until you're ready to frost.

For the brown butter frosting:

- 2 sticks softened salted butter
- 4 oz softened cream cheese
- 4 cups powdered sugar
- 1 tsp vanilla extract

Carrot cake is even better when the flavors have had a chance to develop overnight, allowing it to easily be made a couple days in advance. This cake is quite tender, so you may find it easier to frost layers that have been in the freezer for a few hours, giving them more structure for decorating.

Frosting instructions:

1. Melt one stick of butter in a pan over medium heat. Swirl the butter in the pan occasionally, keeping a watchful eye as the butter starts to bubble up and change color. Once the butter becomes golden, it will quickly turn brown and have a nutty aroma. Turn the heat off before it begins to burn, and set the pan aside until completely cool. Transfer cooled butter to the fridge to solidify just a bit before using.

2. Beat together the remaining stick of butter and cream cheese until smooth. While beating on low, add in your powdered sugar very slowly. Pour in vanilla and browned butter, taking care to scrape any browned bits from the pan (they're full of flavor!), and continue to beat for 4-5 minutes on medium or until light and fluffy. Use immediately or store in the fridge, allowing it to come back to room temp before decorating. Frost and decorate your cake as desired, and store in the fridge before serving.

Pavlovas

for the feast of the Ascension (May 9)

by Marisa Fredrickson

Yields 8 servings.

Ingredients:

- 2/3 cup room-temperature egg whites (about 5 eggs). *Save your yolks for lemon curd!*
- 1 1/4 cup castor sugar (*if you don't have castor, pulse cane sugar in a food processor until it's fine, but not powdered*)
- 2 1/2 tsp corn or arrowroot starch
- 1 tsp white vinegar

Pavlovas are a cloud-like dessert with a crisp exterior and marshmallow center. For best success, avoid a humid environment when baking. Rainy days and stovetop cooking can cause your meringue to become sticky instead of crisp. Making these in the evening and letting them rest overnight is helpful.

Instructions:

1. Preheat oven to 325 degrees. With a hand or stand mixer, beat egg whites on medium/low until foamy. Once foamy, slowly add in sugar one tablespoon at a time. Continue beating your meringue until it is thick, white, and glossy. Test its stability by holding your whisk upside down. If the meringue flops over, keep beating on medium until it is stiff. It is better to increase time than speed. This process takes about 10 minutes.

2. Sprinkle vinegar and starch into your bowl, then beat a few seconds more. Prepare your baking sheet by putting a dab of meringue in each corner, then laying a sheet of parchment on top. This will keep your surface from shifting when forming the pavlovas.

3. Fill a piping bag or ziplock with meringue, then pipe your pavlovas roughly 3" wide and 1 1/2" tall. You can trace a small cup on your parchment for consistency in size as well, just be sure to flip the parchment over so you don't get pencil on your pavlovas.

4. Place your baking sheet in the oven and immediately turn the temp down to 225 degrees. Bake for 1 1/2 hours, or just until the pavlovas are dry and crisp on the outside. Work quickly, as you don't want the oven to lose heat.

5. Allow the pavlovas to rest in the oven, door closed, until they are completely cool. Two hours or overnight is ideal. If you aren't serving right away, store them in a covered container on the counter for up to 24 hours. Just before serving, top with lemon curd and whipped cream.

Lemon Curd:

- 4 egg yolks
- 1/2 cup sugar
- 1/3 cup fresh lemon juice
- Zest from 1 lemon
- 6 Tbsp salted butter

Instructions:

1. Fill a saucepan with a couple inches of water and set over medium high heat.

2. Combine juice, yolks, zest, and sugar in a glass or metal bowl.

3. Place the bowl on top of your steaming water, whisking continuously for 5 minutes, or until the curd has thickened quite a bit.

4. Allow the curd to cool on your counter. Cover with plastic wrap, letting the wrap touch the surface so that a skin doesn't form, and refrigerate.

Whipped Cream:

- 3/4 cup cold heavy whipping cream
- 1 tsp vanilla
- 1/2 Tbsp powdered sugar *(optional)*

The unsweetened cream pairs well with the sugary pavlova, but feel free to sweeten yours if you'd like!

The Case for Growing Flowers

by Virginia Elmer

Holy Recreation. This is a concept someone introduced to me a long time ago that I have had to ponder. It basically means this: all that we do in a day should be done in the name of Jesus, for the glory of God. This includes our rest! And, because so much of our path to sanctity consists in fulfilling exactly the duties in our state of life, our rest should actually be ordered towards work: we rest so that we may work more faithfully and energetically in the service of God. Our hobbies are an important part of this rest since they are not strictly "duties." I would argue that cultivating intentional hobbies is crucial. Here are a few things that can happen when we aren't intentional about this:

First, when we are left with free time, sometimes unexpected free time, we spend that time in a way that either does not fulfill our duties or in a way that doesn't allow us the rest needed to fulfill our duties later. For example, many of us, when gifted a few blessed minutes of quiet, can tend to throw ourselves on the couch and mindlessly start to scroll on our phone. The next thing we know, thirty minutes have passed, our littles need us again or it's time to start dinner, and we have spent that time neither working nor resting. We are just as tired as before, and we will have nothing to show for that time that we will never get back. There are many, many warnings in our Catholic tradition about the dangers of idleness. "Time is as precious as heaven," says St. Bernard. But when we are intentional about cultivating hobbies, we have things to fill those hours (or minutes!) that are either restful or tend to the duties of our vocation — or both!

The second thing that can happen without this reservoir of hobbies to draw from in between our hours of labor is we can choose the *wrong* hobbies. We can choose hobbies that drain us instead of refresh us, that require too much time or energy away from our vocation, or that are even occasions of sin for us. Or we can simply let the world and the anti-Catholic culture choose hobbies for us, like with social media or the latest show to binge watch. On the other hand, when we are intentional about our hobbies, we can choose hobbies that are truly restful to the mind or the body, leave us with a tangible skill that we can bring to our families as homemakers, help us to fight idleness and anxiety, and actually grow us in virtue.

> "It is with the smallest brushes that the artist
> paints the most exquisitely beautiful pictures."
>
> — St. Andre Bessette

A few examples of this might include: decorating the home, painting or drawing, photography, playing an instrument, singing, sewing, learning a language, sourdough and other baking, canning, writing, reading edifying books, supportive exercising, nature walks or observations, and, the one I want to talk to you about today ... flower gardening!

There are lots of ways to flower garden. You can focus on annuals, similar to or even alongside growing vegetables. You can focus on perennials and annuals for your landscape, containers, or even a Mary garden. You can grow them for looks, you can grow them for cut flower arrangements in your home, or you can grow them for medicinal purposes.

If you've never grown flowers before, here is the gist of what it consists of:

Planting Preparation: Before you ever plant a thing, you do have some preparatory work to do. From requiring the least work to the most, here are your options for planting: a pre-existing bed, like a flower bed around your house; containers or raised beds (for these, you just need to buy containers and dirt!); or starting a new bed or garden from scratch, which requires extensive preparation, like tilling, using one of the no-till methods growing in popularity, putting down landscape paper, amending the soil with compost, removing sod, or applying mulch. You also have to pay close attention to the light in your bed, so that you can choose the right plant to go there.

Growing: You can start to grow flowers two ways: by seed or with an existing plant. The existing plants can come from a friend dividing their own plants or can be bought at the store.

Maintenance: While the plant is growing, it will need food, water, and light. Each plant has different requirements for all three categories, so make sure you do your research on what you are growing. Plants can also be susceptible to pests, fungus, and diseases, which might need to be prevented or addressed. You will also need to weed and mulch around your plant.

Harvesting: This again depends on your goals! If your plants are merely ornamental, you will want all the blooms to stay right where they are on the plant. In this case, the only work you might need to do is deadheading, cutting back in the winter (possibly), and dividing (possibly). If you want the blooms for arrangements (fresh or dried), medicinal purposes, or seeds, you will want to get to know your plant and make sure you are cutting at the right time of day, the right way, and at the right life cycle in the plant, as this varies from flower to flower. As you can see, it is a hobby that varies widely and can be as simple or as complex as you would like it to be. A full flower garden or cut-flower production is quite different from a few flowers in pots on your front porch, but any of them can be restful to the mind, invigorating to the body, and tend towards your vocation.

Introduction to Floral Arranging

Words and Photos by Emily Malloy

A sound dances through the air and betrays the joyful, rambunctious child's play in the next room. The smell of tonight's roast fills the remaining spaces of the house. My eyes rest on the most fragile and delicate of God's creation: flowers spilling out of a vase. Our homes contain countless examples of God's creative and merciful genius in a series of beautiful, fleeting moments. Yet, of all that God freely gives, there is something unique about the gift of the flower. Flowers possess within them the unique ability to bring joy and facilitate a sense of wonder and humility because of their fleeting beauty. A marvel of nature is its capacity to draw us toward our shared Creator. It forces us to press the brakes on our ever-quickening pace of life to savor the present moment, the greatest place to ponder God. Flowers are a visual sign of our cooperation with God in the garden, yet they are gifts from God in and of themselves. Paradoxically, the fruits of nature are at the mercy of the same forces of nature that also sustain them, a reality that produces both awe of the delicate perseverance of flowers and the precarious equilibrium of creation. The most inspiring of all realities of the earth is that even the rose in her dainty splendor is not made in the likeness of her Creator — a beautiful reminder of God's love for those who are.

We participate in God's creation in an extraordinary way by inviting the garden into our homes, providing a gift for all who encounter the beauty. During our busy days, flowers enable us to pause to marvel in God's perfect design and provision. Floral design is an art form in which the Creator is a custodian of beauty. We aren't able to will a flower seed into existence, nor can we take credit for the rain or sun which sustains it. We can, however, arrange the entire landscape into the scope of a vase. Of the mediums of artists, floral arranging is one in which the designer remains in a posture of awe in the momentary and haunting beauty of a bloom. The flower and arrangement that contains it is unrepeatable. The designer seeks to cooperate with its unique and unrepeatable characteristics while the flowers are still fresh. But how do we replicate the beauty of the garden into something the home can contain? There is a simple recipe in floral design that can be followed for every arrangement and container shape.

It is beautiful to create arrangements that call to mind the gardens within which they grew. Those that beckon and inspire us with their layers of texture, color, and shapes. Each flower in the garden plays its part to form a symphony. We seek to recreate a microcosm of this same symphony within a vase. This aesthetic, known as garden design, made a resurgence over the last decade from the more "polished" and rounded designs of days past. This style is heavily dependent upon greenery and asymmetry to create a look that mimics the garden; driven by the personality and shape of each flower, as opposed to forcing a flower to conform to a rounded, ball shape. These steps will uniformly apply to any container used.

When establishing the composition of a flower arrangement, one must think of it like the creation of any work that can be done in stages. There are four basic layers in floral design: focal flowers (autumnal examples being hydrangea, mums, roses, dahlias, etc.), filler flowers (hypericum, asters, spray roses, etc.), foliage (evergreens, coral bells, dusty miller, eucalyptus, etc.), and airy finishes (grasses, Queen Anne's lace, sea holly, craspedia, etc.). There can often be lots of crossing over in the layers of blooms. Filler flowers can take the shape of a focal in an arrangement. Some focal flowers (when outshined by other fantastical blooms — hello: Itoh peonies) can take on a supporting role. Some branchier forms of flowers can build to form a wonderful structure. There can also be layers within the layers: several types of fillers, greens, and accents. It is key to take note of the flowers you are working with and how they best fit the needed roles.

A flower arrangement is first created by establishing a foundation or structure, typically consisting of greens or foliage. These stems set the tone of the overall arrangement. Arrange in different heights and angles (all making sure that the stems are in water), calling to mind the beautiful asymmetry of the landscape. Make use of a lot of greens — the designs feel more whimsical and there is always more than enough to find! After the stage has been set by the greenery, it is time to make a home for the star of the show: focal flowers. There will be obvious gaps and pockets made available by the foliage for these large-headed blooms. Work in groupings of one, two, and three to create a visual balance. Commonly, these showy flowers consist of the least number of stems in an arrangement. Be sure to create depth and interest by placing flowers at different heights within the vase.

After the large flowers have been placed, it is time for the filler. Filler flowers hold an important place in an arrangement. They draw our eye to the focals and connect them to create cohesion in the design. They also add the depth and texture. Last, and far from least, are the additions of airy stems. These light, whimsical flowers finish off the design and create drama. Their placement is decided by their unique shape and form — the more bended and interesting the stem, the better. It is this layer that adds the organic and natural element in garden-style arrangements.

On vases: Vessels are my favorite part of floral design and, in my opinion, are just as important as the flowers themselves. Chicken or the egg? Does the container dictate the number of flowers needed or do the flowers dictate the vase? As with anything, it depends upon perspective! One thing is certain, wider-mouthed containers (think urns) require more flowers than a smaller-mouthed one. A table centerpiece is a 360-degree design that requires more flowers than an arrangement that will be placed up against a wall.

On the hunt: As with any hunting conquest, foraging for flowers is a fantastic thrill! They are cultivated by the wild and are undoubtedly unique in their form. Because of this, I always keep a pair of clippers in my car. An important aspect of foraging (aside from ensuring you're not trespassing) is being able to identify what is being cut. I highly recommend keeping the Seek from iNaturalist on your phone for quick identification as you do not want to come home with an armload of poison ivy. Foraging can be as simple as collecting a few stems of roadside wildflowers or something interesting at your property's edge. Don't be shy — if you see something lovely on a neighbor's property, they are likely to share the bounty! Regardless of where you are foraging, it is always good practice to be meager in the amount you cut.

On sourcing: The best place to source flowers is your own garden! However, many small flower shops and grocery stores have fantastic offerings to delight any home. Home and garden centers are also great sources for flowers: cut some stems off and plant what remains to enjoy cutting for years to come!

Tips: If you feel that you don't have enough flowers for your wide-mouthed urn, don't be afraid to add layers of interesting greens to fill out the space. One walk through your yard is likely to produce lots of interesting foliage options to fill any holes in the design. And if an arrangement feels overcrowded, there is no shame in removing a few stems to give flowers more space. Editing often produces even more beautiful arrangements. Or you can utilize the full space available within the container — blend the space between the vessel and blooms to have the appearance of a cohesive unit. So, do not be afraid to have flowers grazing the lip of the vase or drooping a bit below.

FELIX CULPA

Resurrection and the Theology of the Body

By Mackenzie Worthing

"Jesus said to her, 'I am the resurrection and the life; he who believes in me,
though he die, yet shall he live, and whoever lives and believes in me shall never die.
Do you believe this?'"

— John 11:25-26

One of the most beautiful liturgical moments of the entire year is the proclamation of the Exultet at the Easter Vigil. During this incredible song of praise we are reminded of the glory and splendor of Christ's triumph over sin and death. In it, we hear how all of Heaven resounds with glory and the earth trembles in joyful anticipation of the fullness of redemption. We are reminded of the *felix culpa*, the "happy fault" of Adam which gained for us so "great, so glorious a Redeemer." Fortunately for us, Adam's fault was not only corrected, but Jesus' salvific action gained for us something even greater than the life enjoyed by Adam and Eve in the Garden. When created, man was in harmony with God, with himself, with others, and with all of creation. Sin disrupted all of these relationships. We all know what the fallout of these disrupted relationships can look like: distance from God, health issues, struggling against temptation, anxiety or depression, miscommunication with loved ones, rejection from others, the lack of proper care for creation — the list goes on for however many sins, sorrows, and sufferings there can be in this fallen world. Christ's Resurrection makes it possible for all these relationships to not only be restored, but to be glorified on the last day. We know very well what it is for our body and soul to be in conflict with one another, but the Resurrection of Christ points us to the final day when body and soul will be united with such integrity we can hardly imagine what it will be like.

Christ, fully God and fully man, was alone capable of closing the divide between God and man. His death on the Cross was the consummation of salvation history — of God's desire to draw man back to Himself. But He did more than pay the debt — He crossed the threshold of death as a conquerer and became the first to rise from the dead to a new and more glorious life. In death, His body and soul were separated and experienced that consequence of the fall. But then, in the Resurrection, His soul was rejoined to His body but yet more glorious. His resurrected body was like His body before, but also was different somehow in an almost indefinable way. His Resurrection demonstrates that death is not the end for man, nor is man meant to continue as a bodiless soul for eternity. For man, made of both body and soul, is meant to be body and soul in the life to come.

St. Paul states in his first letter to the Corinthians that "Christ has been raised from the dead, the first fruits of those who have fallen asleep. For as by a man came death, by a man has come also the resurrection of the dead. For as in Adam all die, so also in Christ shall all be made alive" (15:20-21). In Adam all physically die and all are subject to spiritual death. We struggle in this world against temptation. Our bodies and souls may still be united but they do not often cooperate. We have access to His abundant grace and we still experience temptation and still struggle even if we are in the habit of virtue. Through the Resurrection of the new Adam, all who believe in Him have hope for the complete integration of body and soul. The original harmony of the garden will be restored but also made better — not only will man's body and soul no longer struggle with one another, but they shall be united in a harmonious, glorious way that does not appear to have been the portion of Adam.

St. John Paul II's *Theology of the Body* is famous for its beautiful exposition on Adam and Eve in the garden and God's original design for man, but he also muses with St. Paul on the body in regards to the resurrection. He states Paul's understanding of the triumph of Christ in this profound way: "One can say that St. Paul sees the future resurrection as a certain *restitutio in integrum*, that is, as the reintegration and at the same time as the attainment of the fullness of humanity. ... [it] can only be an *introduction to a new fullness*. It will be a fullness that presupposes man's whole history, formed by the drama of the tree of the knowledge of good and evil and at the same time permeated by the mystery of redemption" (72:3). The general resurrection, then, when all will be reunited body and soul on the last day, will not only be a restoration to the Garden of Eden, but it will be a fullness of the human person formed by the story of salvation history. Christ's resurrected body bears the wounds of His Crucifixion — His glorious body was formed by His salvific act! If many of us long for things to be as they were in the Garden while yet here on earth, how much more must we truly long for the general resurrection! How much more beautiful will it be to have complete and glorious integrity of body and soul and all the history of man's redemption imprinted on man, as well as our suffering for the sake of such a kingdom?

This understanding of the resurrection ought to form us day to day. It is, after all, the foundation of our hope. How can we anticipate the world to come in the world we live in now with so many daily reminders of how disparate the body and the soul are? John Paul II suggests, "The Pauline anthropology of the resurrection is cosmic and universal together: everyone bears in himself the image of Adam, and everyone is also called to bear in himself the image of Christ, the image of the Risen One. ... It is a reality implanted in the man of 'this world,' maturing in him toward the final fulfillment" (71:4). We are called to remember that we bear the image of the Risen One within ourselves already by virtue of our baptism. We are called to submit our whole selves, body and soul, to Christ and the pursuit of holiness for the sake of the Kingdom. He asks nothing less than our whole selves — He desires us, body and soul, to be committed to Him. Remembering that we belong to Him, that we have staked our hope for eternity in His life, will help us mature towards the fulfillment of Christ's promises.

As St. Paul reminds us, "Do you not know that your body is a temple of the Holy Spirit within you, which you have from God? You are not your own; you were bought with a price. So glorify God in your body" (1 Corinthians 6:19-20). Our bodies are not our own. When we mistakenly act as if they are, that is when we stray from the Lord and when we are in danger of not living life abundant with Him in the world to come. St. Paul is emphatic that we must remember the price that was paid for us and give ourselves to the glory of God. We glorify God with our bodies in lots of different ways, but primarily in the ways that work towards the union of body and soul: submitting our bodies to moderation when struggling against temptations of the flesh, eating well and getting adequate sleep, dressing with intention and modesty, praying in attitudes that remind us what we are doing, fasting and abstaining as the liturgical season or personal devotion requires, respecting the bodies of others and tending to their souls as charity of heart and personal responsibility demand as wives, mothers, teachers, friends, sisters, daughters, etc. We are tasked with conducting ourselves, body and soul, in such a way that reminds ourselves, and others, of the resurrected Christ. May we truly long for the return of Christ and look forward to the glory that awaits those who love and serve Him. *Christus Resurrexit, sicut dixit, alleluia!*

Ways to Cultivate a Remembrance of the Resurrection:

1. Set aside time to reflect on the Exultet on Holy Saturday.
2. Offer up struggles with health for those who do not share the hope of the resurrection.
3. Strive for union in body and soul by working on rooting out your primary vice.
4. Celebrate the joy of Easter in special ways throughout the season with a focus on using the body and the soul to glorify God: making special treats with your family, taking a hike for the Ascension, having a bonfire at Pentecost, reading a good book with a friend, etc.

"If the Spirit of him who raised Jesus from the dead dwells in you,
he who raised Christ Jesus from the dead will give life to your mortal
bodies also through his Spirit who dwells in you."

— Romans 8:11

Sun Tea

for the feast of Our Lady of Fatima (May 13) and the miracle of the sun

by Marisa Fredrickson

Lemon Chamomile

- 8 cups water
- 1/2 cup chamomile
- 1 lemon sliced

Hibiscus Rose and Raspberry

- 8 cups water
- 1/2 cup dried hibiscus
- 2 Tbsp dried rose petals or hips
- 1 cup fresh raspberries

Instructions:

1. Combine all ingredients in a half-gallon jar.

2. Seal the top with a lid and place in a safe spot outdoors or in a sunny window for 2 hours.

3. Strain, sweeten with honey if desired, and serve over ice.

SUMMER

To understand what summer should look like, we need to briefly take a look at fall, winter, and spring. We are beings called to live in seasons (and, oh there are so many kinds of seasons!). Autumn is our time of winding down, winter is a period of rest, and spring is the renewal. Summer is where we may reap the fruits of the whole process. It is naturally a busier and fuller season for most of us, and the interior work done the rest of the year helps prepare us for all the activity.

But for many of us, living seasonally in this way — with how we direct our energy — can be a challenge. Winter might have been full of sickness, mothers may be drained, those in school may feel mentally exhausted, there may be endless house projects, unemployment, moving, relationship challenges, and so forth. Summer might be a relief in some ways, but our capacity for abundance may be limited.

We're all living and learning. The beauty of seasons is that they happen over and over. And every new season is an opportunity to begin again. Maybe this summer God is calling you to rest. No matter how busy our external circumstances have us, we can all rest in the Lord. Even on the busiest days, our hearts can hide away in Jesus' Sacred Heart, and receive their fill from the Source. As we enter into this new summer, we pray that you are able to take care and tend amidst the flurry of life. To your home, to your garden, to your family, to your health, to your soul.

"Praise, you servants of the Lord,
Praise the name of the Lord.
Blessed be the name of the Lord
Both now and forever.
From the rising of the sun to its setting,
Let the name of the Lord be praised."

— Psalm 113:1-3

summer

EMBER DAYS

"For in Him we live and move and have our being."

— Acts 17:28

While many of us may not be farmers, we should all desire to live more fully in reliance on God's care and provision in our lives. As we step into a season that tends to have full schedules and high energy, let us set aside time to examine ourselves in light of our Creator. May the words our Father taught us be ever on our lips as we pray, "give us this day our daily bread."

The summer Ember Days, or Pentecost Ember Days, take place the week after Pentecost (on the traditional calendar) near the summer solstice. This Embertide calls to mind the harvest of wheat — and more specifically as wheat is used for the Eucharist — and the fire of Pentecost.

Since many ordinations take place this time of year, it is appropriate to offer fasting and prayer for those men to be ordained in your diocese.

"Graciously pour into our souls, we beseech Thee, O Lord,

Thy Holy Spirit, by Whose wisdom we are created and by

Whose providence we are governed."

— Collect from Ember Saturday in the Octave of Pentecost

what's in season?

SUMMER

Vegetables

- Bell peppers
- Cucumbers
- Green beans
- Green onions
- Lettuce
- Okra
- Radishes
- Summer squash
- Tomatoes
- Zucchini

Fruits

- Blackberries
- Blueberries
- Cantaloupe
- Cherries
- Figs
- Mangos
- Melon
- Nectarines
- Peaches
- Plums
- Rhubarb
- Raspberries
- Strawberries

The beauty of seasonal eating is that nature often provides the nutrients needed for that particular season. The summertime is inarguably the easiest season to eat seasonally because there is so much abundance and variety in produce available, even if you're buying it locally! For example, there are so many hydrating and mineral-rich fruits to get you through the hustle and bustle of summertime and the minerals you'll naturally lose through sweat. It's a great time to take advantage of all of the color at the farmers market or grocery store and fill the plates of you and your loved ones with as much variety as you can!

Summer Appetizers

Summer charcuterie board ideas:

- Peaches
- Watermelon
- Cucumbers
- Cherries
- Cherry tomatoes
- Sourdough crackers
- Brie cheese
- Mozzarella cheese
- Walnuts
- Prosciutto
- Salami
- Fig jam

Beet hummus:

- 1-2 small beets
- 15 oz cooked chickpeas *(soaked first is best!)*
- 1 clove garlic
- 2 Tbsp olive oil
- Juice from 1/2 lemon
- 1/2 tsp sea salt

Boil beets (skin on) until fork tender. When ready to use, peel the skin off and chop into chunks. Add all ingredients to a food processor until desired texture.

Frozen grapes & yogurt dip:

- Grapes of choice
- 1 cup yogurt*
- 2 Tbsp heavy cream
- 2 Tbsp collagen
- 1 tsp maple syrup

Freeze grapes (of your choice) for 4 hours. Whip heavy cream with an electric whisk/mixer, and then stir into yogurt with collagen and maple syrup. Use toothpicks to dip frozen grapes into the dip. You can try dipping the frozen grapes into the yogurt mixture and freezing on parchment paper for individual servings of yogurt-dipped grapes.

Note: You can use Greek yogurt, but a higher protein yogurt like skyr would also work well.

Butter-dipped radishes:

- 20-30 radishes
- 2 sticks butter
- Sea salt

Thoroughly wash/scrub radishes (keep greens on if you'd like). Gently melt butter over the stove until it is a mayo consistency, and then dip the radishes. Lay on a parchment paper-lined baking sheet (or in a glass container), sprinkle sea salt over them, and then leave in the fridge for 20-30 minutes to set. Serve right away!

Summer Appetizers II

Melon & mozzarella salad:

- 1 cantaloupe
- 1 honeydew melon
- 2 cups blueberries
- 1.5 cups mozzarella balls
- 1 cup fresh basil leaves
- 1.5 Tbsp olive oil
- Juice of 1 lemon
- 1 tsp honey
- Sea salt

Scoop melon into balls and mix with blueberries and mozzarella. Whisk olive oil, lemon, and honey together, pour over fruit/cheese and toss. Add sea salt to taste.

Note: Get creative with food options based on what you have. Swap figs for blueberries or watermelon for cantaloupe/honeydew. Add balsamic glaze instead of the olive oil mixture. Use mint either in place of or with basil. Add sliced prosciutto into the mix, or some chopped nuts. Mix with arugula for that true salad feel.

Prosciutto-wrapped Cantaloupe:

- 1 cantaloupe
- 5 oz prosciutto (sliced thin)
- 2-3 Tbsp honey-balsamic glaze
- Fresh basil to top

Cut the cantaloupe into wedges. Wrap the prosciutto around the wedges and set on a plate/platter. Drizzle the glaze over top.

Oyster crackers:

- 2 cans smoked oysters (in olive oil), drained
- 2 oz sharp cheddar cheese, sliced thin
- Sourdough crackers (or crackers of your choice!)
- Hot/buffalo sauce to taste

Drain oysters of oil and set aside. Slice cheese and place on crackers. Place an oyster on each cracker, and drizzle sauce over top.

Oysters can be tricky for people to take a liking to, but they are so nutrient-dense that we should make an effort to get them on rotation. Of course, if you have access to fresh oysters that will always be better. But if not, these make a great snack!

IHS
LIBER VITÆ

BREATH

Some of the most beautiful things in this life are felt like a deep breath for the soul. A still, quiet cathedral with light pouring in, incense drifting out an open window, a walk on a crisp summer morning, the breeze on our skin, the rustle of the leaves, the songs of the birds. The Hebrew word *ruach* is used throughout the Old Testament to mean spirit, breath, or wind. The first mention is in just the second verse of Genesis, "and the earth was without form or shape, with darkness over the abyss and a mighty wind sweeping over the waters." *Pneuma* is an ancient Greek word for breath used in the New Testament to describe the Holy Spirit. The third Person of the Trinity, referred to as the Breath of God, is our constant intercessor and comforter. When our Lord was resurrected and returned to meet His friends, John writes, "Jesus said to them again, "Peace be with you. As the Father has sent me, even so I am sending you." And when he had said this, *he breathed on them and said to them, "Receive the Holy Spirit"* (20:21-22).

We know that along with a relationship with the Trinity, deep breathing is supportive to our overall well-being. Breathing is like a power switch for our nervous system and its two branches — parasympathetic and sympathetic. Your parasympathetic nervous system stimulates rest, calm, and healing. The sympathetic branch of your nervous system is what your body uses during times of stress to direct blood flow to the organs that need it most — like your muscles and brain, but away from other organs like those of your digestive system. According to author James Nestor in his book *Breath: The New Science of a Lost Art,* "The lungs are covered with nerves that extend to both sides of the autonomic nervous system, and many of the nerves that connect to the parasympathetic system are located in the lower lobes, which is one of the reasons long and slow breaths are so relaxing. As molecules of breath descend deeper, they switch on parasympathetic nerves, which send more messages for the organs to rest and digest. As air ascends through the lungs during exhalation, the molecules stimulate an even more powerful parasympathetic response. The deeper and more softly we breathe in, and the longer we exhale, the more slowly the heart beats and the calmer we become."

"Breathe in me, O Holy Spirit, that my thoughts may all be holy.

Act in me, O Holy Spirit, that my work, too, may be holy.

Draw my heart, O Holy Spirit, that I love but what is holy.

Strengthen me, O Holy Spirit, to defend all that is holy.

Guard me, then, O Holy Spirit, that I always may be holy."

— St. Augustine

In contrast to this, he writes on the sympathetic nervous system, "A profusion of nerves to this system are spread out at the top of the lungs. When we take short, hasty breaths, the molecules of air switch on the sympathetic nerves.... The more messages the system gets, the bigger the emergency."

Nestor's book also explores the ways prayer and meditation are weaved through different cultures and religions. He writes that most calming, repetitive prayers come in waves of about 6 seconds. The "ideal" inhale and exhale for good health is apparently about 5.5 seconds each, which helps to balance the levels of carbon dioxide and oxygen in the blood. For us Catholics, the first and second parts to the Hail Mary on our Rosary beads often each clock in at about 6 seconds each. This is a beautiful testament to the gift the Lord has given us in this ritual, a support for health and peace for the soul.

There has been a resurgence in recent years of attention to mouth breathing versus nose breathing, which is an important thing to highlight when speaking about this topic. While nose breathing and mouth taping — yes, taping your mouth shut while you sleep — is trendy right now, it is actually age-old wisdom. In the mid-1800's, a lawyer-turned-painter named George Catlin ventured to the American west to document the lives of Native American tribes. He painted hundreds of portraits of them and their striking characteristics — wide jaws with plenty of room for teeth, good bone structure, tall, strong, and striking. Chronic health problems were very sparse. The tribes attributed much of their good health to a "great secret of life": breathing. They explained that breath inhaled through the mouth took strength from the body, caused stress and disease, and deformed the face. Breath inhaled through the nose, they believed, did the opposite. Catlin wrote that mothers in all of the tribes would close baby's mouth after feeding and if it drifted open while they slept. This practice, he wrote, "was as old and unchanging as the hills."

There is actually more and more modern science coming out to support these old wives' tales, with doctors like Dr. Mark Burhenne. He writes there that, "Your gut health, brain health, and even sleep quality are intimately tied to the health of your teeth and gums, and one cannot be improved without addressing the other." Dr. Burhenne has been studying mouth breathing for decades and its impacts on overall health. According to his research, mouth breathing can cause abnormal facial growth and development, misaligned teeth, sleep issues, poor mental processing and fatigue, and overall worse health. He writes on his blog that breathing through the mouth actually deprives the body of nitric oxide because your body produces 25 percent of this in the sinuses. Nitric oxide has been shown to

"A soul in which the Holy Spirit dwells is never weary in the presence of God;

his heart gives forth a breath of love."

— St. John Vianney

improve sleep quality, regulate the inflammatory response, enhance memory and learning, and more. Many things contribute to a tendency to mouth breathe, which might include sinus issues that need to be revised, lip or tongue ties/tight fascia in the body, or, according to Dr. Weston Price, lack of sufficient fat-soluble vitamins in the diets of generations preceding ours. This is all something to keep in mind when seeking overall wellness for yourself and your family. All that to say, we ask the Holy Spirit to breathe new life into our souls each and every one of our days.

"The Spirit of God has made me;

the breath of the Almighty gives me life."

—Job 33:4

Ordinary Time

Summer is a time when the spirit is full. The warm weather often means more community gatherings, playdates at the park, dinners outside, maybe even an easier time getting to daily Mass. In my experience, it also is a time more conducive to order. Sure, for many there's the busyness that actually may make this more of a challenge. But I see longer days, with peaceful mornings and calmer evenings. I find myself drawn more to uniting my morning prayer with setting my circadian rhythm on my doorstep. Getting in that morning sun while drawing closer to the Son through the Word. Full days of outdoor activity prepare my kids for a more docile evening, inclining them to be [somewhat] present to the Rosary. I don't see this order as a coincidence — for it is *ordinary* time, where we embrace the natural rhythm of life. The word *ordinalis* means numbered or ruled. While it does not have the intense feel of Advent, Christmas, Lent, or Easter, ordinary time is where we should be seeing the fruits of our concentrated fasting and feasting. Ordinary time is a period of growth and subtle transformation in our spiritual lives. Many of us are very intentional with our spiritual practices in the major seasons, but then relax a bit when the green vestments come out. A challenge for us all would be to not simply let ordinary time pass us by, but to embrace the richness the Church has set out for us in these many weeks and months. Let's evaluate our current spiritual routines and practices and discern where the Lord may be calling us to grow. This could also be a good time to look at the calendar and see how we can mark this season. Do you have special devotions you pray throughout the year? What practices could you take up during this time?

- Marian Consecration
- Seven Sundays Devotion to St. Joseph
- First Saturday Devotion
- First Friday Devotion
- Consecration to St. Joseph
- 30-day novena to St. Joseph
- Your favorite novenas
- Choose three feast days to really celebrate in summer
- Host a Sacred Heart party
- Gather friends for a bonfire on the nativity of St. John the Baptist (June 24th), and use this opportunity to burn old blessed goods
- Curate a summer list of spiritual books you've been thinking about for years (better yet, grab the ones off your bookshelf that haven't been opened)
- Host a Lord's Day celebration in your home, inviting friends & family

Summer Berry Roulade

by Marisa Fredrickson

This lightly sweet rolled cake is surprisingly simple, and impressively beautiful. Edible flowers sprinkled on top add a special touch. Calendula, cornflower, honeysuckle, and marigolds are just a few to consider!

For the sponge cake:

- 4 room-temperature eggs
- 2/3 cup sugar
- Pinch of sea salt
- 1 cup all-purpose flour*
- 1/2 tsp baking powder
- 2 Tbsp whole milk
- 3 Tbsp coconut or avocado oil
- 1 tsp white vinegar
- 2 tsp vanilla extract
- Powdered sugar, for dusting

**If making gluten-free, consider making 1.5x the recipe, as the baked cake will be quite thin otherwise.*

Instructions:

1. Preheat oven to 350 degrees. Prepare a jelly roll or sheet pan by lining it with parchment paper and oiling any exposed edges. Place eggs in a bowl and beat on high until they double in volume. Slowly sprinkle in the sugar and continue beating until the mixture is pale, thick, and greatly increased in volume. This can take a minimum of 5 minutes.

2. Whisk together all wet ingredients, then gently stir into the egg mixture. Sift together flour and baking powder over the eggs, then whisk by hand until just combined. Scrape the bowl with a spatula to ensure everything is incorporated, then pour the batter into your prepared pan.

3. Bake for about 12 minutes. If your cake springs back when gently touched, it is finished baking. Overbaking can lead to cracks and a dry texture.

4. Sift powdered sugar over the surface of your warm cake, then invert the cake onto a tea towel, sugared side down. Gently peel off the parchment paper, then roll your cake with the towel and allow to cool.

For the filling:

- 8 oz Mascarpone
- 8 oz heavy whipping cream
- 1 Tbsp maple syrup or honey
- 1 tsp vanilla
- Fresh berries, *for topping*

Instructions:

1. Whip together all of the ingredients on medium-high speed until it becomes very thick and fluffy and leaves tracks in the cream.

2. Carefully unroll your cooled cake. Spread the whipped filling across the surface of the cake, leaving 1/2" at the very end of the roll so it doesn't squeeze out.

3. Slice berries so they aren't too large, and sprinkle evenly across the surface. Carefully roll your cake up, ending seam-side down.

4. Wrap your roulade in cling wrap and refrigerate for at least an hour, or up to 2 days. Top as desired and serve.

Living Extraordinary Virtue in the Midst of an Ordinary Life
Zélie and Louis Martin

By Mackenzie Worthing

In the middle of the summer of 1858, Louis Martin and Zélie Guerin wed. They had not followed the usual course of meeting and marrying in the early years of adulthood; in fact Louis was 35 and Zélie 27 when they wed, which might seem more normal these days but was less common at the time. Louis had intended to become a monk but could not succeed in his Latin. Zélie had desired to be a Sister of Charity but could not keep up with the lifestyle due to a few health concerns. After leaving the dream of the monastery, Louis became a watchmaker. After leaving the hope of the convent, Zélie dedicated herself to the craft of lacemaking. They met on a bridge in Alençon, where divine intervention enlightened Zélie that she had just passed by her future husband. Little did they know what their married life would bring, though they clearly were devoted to God and desired to do His will.

Part of the married vocation is the call to bring children into the world, and the Martins were able to fulfill this call amply. We might be aware of their youngest child, St. Thérèse, the Little Flower and Doctor of the Church. But the Martins actually had nine children in total, only five girls of whom survived childhood. This is part of their story of extraordinary virtue in the midst of an ordinary life: the loss of four beloved children. Although the death of children was pretty common in the course of human history before the last century, Louis and Zélie bore the loss of their little ones with great courage and hope in divine providence. Three of the four died from illness. The last child who died was the baby born to them before Thérèse — another little girl called Marie-Melanie-Thérèse who died essentially from starvation. Zélie had been unable to breastfeed several of her previous children (she was already having complications with the breast cancer that would kill her) and had to give her little ones to a wet nurse who lived a distance from them. Unfortunately, this wet nurse was an alcoholic and was neglecting the baby. They brought her home in hopes of saving her, but the baby died of malnutrition. Marie-Françoise-Thérèse, who we know as St. Thérèse, would be born three years later. From *A Call to a Deeper Love* (the letters of Zélie and Louis Martin), we see that Zélie wrote about the torment of handing over her daughter Thérèse to a wet nurse after her last baby had died of malnutrition. She had tried feeding Thérèse herself for a couple of months, but she was quickly sick, "I quickly knelt at the feet of St. Joseph and asked him for mercy, that the little one be cured, resigning myself completely to the will of God if He wanted to take her. I don't cry often, but I cried while I was praying. ...What consoles me is knowing that God wants it this way, since I did everything I could to raise her myself. So I have nothing to reproach myself for in this regard."

What else we can see of Zélie and Louis' virtues in their letters comes through in their descriptions of normal family life — the funny antics their children devised, the Masses and holy conferences they attended, their devotion to their family rising above their devotion to their work, and the many illnesses each endured and offered to the Lord. We also get a glimpse into the tenderness of their married love. In a letter written while Zélie visited relatives in another city she wrote, "I'm longing to be near you, my dear Louis. I love you with all of my heart, and I feel my affection so much more when you're not here with me. It would be impossible for me to live apart from you." Though we only have a handful of extant letters from Louis, those we have are largely from the years following Zélie's death. One such letter summarizes his insight into how their family was indeed hugely blessed by the Lord: "I want to tell you, my dear children, that I have the urgent desire to thank God and to make you thank God because I feel that our family, though very humble, has the honor of being among the privileged of our adorable Creator."

The virtue that truly seems to characterize Zélie and Louis is one of detachment — detachment from the things of the world and detachment to their own ideas of what their lives ought to look like. Though they prayed to God for certain things, though they longed for all their children to be healthy and well, and though they longed and prayed for Zélie to be cured of her breast cancer, they abandoned themselves to divine providence at the end of the day. The final letters of Zélie's life really bring out her resignation to do whatever it is that God asks of her, even if it means dying and leaving her beloved Louis and their daughters. They made several pilgrimages to holy Marian shrines around France to beg Our Lady's intercession for Zélie, but in a letter dated a couple months before her death Zélie wrote to her sister-in-law, "If the Blessed Mother doesn't cure me it's because my time is at an end, and God wants me to rest elsewhere other than on earth."

For most of us, holiness is to be found in the ordinary. Most of us will not encounter extraordinary opportunities for a single moment of extraordinary virtue: martyrdom, saving someone else's life, accepting the stigmata, or receiving visions. The extraordinary experiences of the mystics are beautiful and profound and really call us to wonder at God's amazing providence and power. But God also works among the ordinary. He came into the world in the ordinary way (barring the virginal conception) after all. He became a child and by His presence in a family, He sanctified the ordinariness of family life. Family life became the primary place of growing in virtue. We are all born into some kind of family or another, whether or not it is broken or whole or whether we live with our families or not. But it is the first experience of the human person in learning how to be and interact with others, how to strive for or reject the life of virtue.

It is therefore in the obedience to our daily duty that we are sanctified. It is following the will of God for our life, no matter what joys or sufferings arise, that we are made holy. This was true of Zélie and Louis. People might say they endured extraordinary hardship through losing four children or in Zélie's struggle with breast cancer or in Louis slowly losing his faculties as he aged, but these are in fact ordinary. We will all die. We all know someone who has had cancer. We all know someone who has lost a child or has struggled with infertility. We all have had a grandparent or elderly relative who has lost their faculties. These are great sufferings but are actually rather ordinary parts of living in a fallen world.

What makes Zélie and Louis extraordinary is how they conducted themselves no matter what they were experiencing as a family. They rejoiced over small happinesses with their children. They celebrated the liturgical year with care. They looked forward to time spent with extended family. They did not deny their sorrows but begged the Lord for mercy. At the end of the day, no matter what it brought, they abandoned themselves to divine providence. They continued praying. They went on pilgrimages. They taught their children to love Christ and His Church, so much so that all five surviving daughters became nuns. They loved one another in such a way that all who knew them knew of their tenderness for each other. They lived their lives completely dedicated to accepting whatever the Lord allowed for them to experience. And they blessed Him in joy and in sorrow. They were faithful in the small things, and this in such a way that one daughter became known as the saint of the "Little Way," a Doctor of the Church, and the "greatest saint of modern times." If that is not encouragement enough for spouses and parents to be devoted to growing in holiness together I do not know what is! May we look to Zélie and Louis as models of love, fortitude, and, above all, joyful resignation to the will of God for ourselves and our families.

Ways to Cultivate Virtue in Your Daily Life:
1. Offer joys and sufferings to the Lord throughout the day, as they arise.
2. See if you can add more visits to the Blessed Sacrament somewhere in your schedule, even if inconvenient.
3. Look for small ways to show love to your family members.
4. Be faithful to your duties in your home whether it be cleaning, cooking, gardening, etc. — especially the duties you dislike or drag your feet on.

"Perfection is accomplishing the will of God in a constant and generous fashion. That person, then, is perfect who does at every instant what God wishes. Ask her at any moment what she is doing, and she will always respond: 'That which God wishes.'"

— Monsignor Paul Lejeune

Pesto Garden Bowls

by Marisa Fredrickson

By mid-summer your garden may be brimming with abundance, or have produced just a few random veggies. This simple recipe is an excellent way to tie together the produce you have and turn it into something delicious. While this serves as an excellent side, we love to add grilled and chopped chicken for an easy-to-serve, balanced meal.

For the pesto:

- 2 cups fresh basil leaves, packed
- 1/2 cup freshly grated parmesan
- 1/2 cup extra virgin olive oil
- 1/3 cup pine nuts (walnuts are an inexpensive substitute!)
- 3-4 cloves of garlic
- Salt and pepper to taste

Pesto is traditionally made with fresh basil, though feel free to substitute half of the basil for carrot tops, spinach, radish greens, or other herbs like parsley and mint.

Instructions:

In a blender or food processor, pulse together the basil, nuts, and garlic. Add the parmesan and pulse a few more times. Slowly add in the olive oil and blend until the pesto has a uniform texture. You may need a splash of more olive oil to get the consistency you prefer. Season with salt and pepper, then transfer to a glass jar and refrigerate for up to 1 week.

For the roasted veggies:

Preheat oven to 450 degrees. Gather any vegetables you have on hand, cutting them into uniform pieces, and arrange them on a baking sheet. Drizzle with cooking fat of choice (I love tallow or avocado oil), and sprinkle with salt and pepper. Roast for 30 minutes, or until tender.

Tip: Roots and cruciferous veggies can be roasted together, while more delicate choices like beans, tomatoes, or asparagus should be added just at the end to prevent overcooking.

Pour a few spoonfuls of pesto over the vegetables, and serve immediately.

Summer Salads

Watermelon Cucumber Salad

- 4 cups cubed watermelon
- 2 cucumbers, peeled & sliced
- 1/2 cup feta cheese, crumbled
- 1 Tbsp mint, chopped
- 1 lime, juiced
- 1 tsp sea salt
- *Optional:* drizzle balsamic vinegar and/or extra virgin olive oil

Nutrient highlights: potassium, vitamin C, sodium, calcium, vitamin B2

Pair with: your favorite summer meal OR a protein source for a complete snack

Potato Salad

- 2 cups small red-skinned potatoes, boiled & cooled
- 1 cup homemade mayo *(or favorite store-bought with avocado/MCT/coconut oil)*
- 8 slices thick-cut bacon, chopped
- 1/3 cup chives
- 1 Tbsp sea salt
- *Optional twists:* chipotle, dijon

Nutrient highlights: vitamin C, potassium, B vitamins, selenium, phosphorous

Pair with: additional protein source

Basic Caprese Salad

- 3-4 medium ripe tomatoes, sliced
- 16 oz fresh mozzarella, sliced
- 1/3 cup fresh basil leaves
- 3 Tbsp extra virgin olive oil
- 2 Tbsp balsamic vinegar
- 1 tsp sea salt

Nutrient highlights: calcium, phosphorous, vitamin B12, sodium, potassium, vitamin C

Pair with: a piece of fruit or sourdough

Sauteed Veggie Salad

- 1 zucchini, sliced
- 2 summer squash, sliced
- 2 cups cherry tomatoes, halved
- 1 red onion, roughly chopped
- 1 bunch asparagus, trimmed & cut
- 1 red pepper, chopped
- 2 Tbsp ghee *(more if needed)*
- 1/2 tsp sea salt
- Splash of lemon juice *(or lime)*
- *Optional:* dijon mustard to taste, favorite soft/crumbled cheese

Nutrient highlights: vitamin C, B vitamins, vitamin K, potassium, sodium

Pair with: your favorite protein!

Devotion to the Sacred Heart of Jesus

Devotion to the Sacred Heart of Jesus is perhaps the greatest devotion in the Catholic Church. It honors the very essence of our Lord — His merciful heart so full of love and humility. This devotion calls us to deeper communion with Jesus by inviting us to take refuge in His most Sacred Heart, cloaking ourselves in the deep shelter of God. By loving, honoring, and trusting in the Sacred Heart of Jesus, we console His heart in the most tender of ways. While this devotion has always existed (beginning with Our Lady!), it became widespread through St. Margaret Mary Alacoque, a religious woman of the seventeenth century who received visions from Jesus instructing her in this devotion.

To practice the First Friday Devotion, we must attend Mass and receive Holy Communion on the first Friday of nine consecutive months, with the intention of making reparation for the innumerable offenses committed against our Lord's Sacred Heart. Jesus laid out twelve promises for those who live this devotion.

1. I will give them all the graces necessary in their state of life.
2. I will establish peace in their homes.
3. I will comfort them in all their afflictions.
4. I will be their secure refuge during life, and above all, in death.
5. I will bestow abundant blessings upon all their undertakings.
6. Sinners will find in My Heart the source and infinite ocean of mercy.
7. Lukewarm souls shall become fervent.
8. Fervent souls shall quickly mount to high perfection.
9. I will bless every place in which an image of My Heart is exposed and honored.
10. I will give to priests the gift of touching the most hardened hearts.
11. Those who shall promote this devotion shall have their names written in My Heart.
12. I promise you in the excessive mercy of My Heart that My all powerful love will grant to all those who receive Holy Communion on the First Fridays in nine consecutive months the grace of final perseverance; they shall not die in My disgrace, nor without receiving their sacraments. My divine Heart shall be their safe refuge in this last moment.

Those who complete this devotion are also granted a plenary indulgence by the Church. Finally, don't forget to celebrate the solemnity of the Sacred Heart of Jesus on June 24th!

> "Behold the Heart which has so loved men that it has spared nothing, even
>
> exhausting and consuming itself in testimony of its love."

— Jesus to St. Margaret Mary Alacoque

Rosary Reflections for Summer

by Emily Patteson

Praying the Rosary is a beautiful devotion that the Church offers us to grow closer to the Lord through the help of Our Lady. As we enter into each new season, we can engage with the different seasons of Jesus' life. During this summer season of ordinary time, we reflect on the Luminous mysteries. These mysteries mark the most "ordinary" time of Jesus' life, but we are encouraged to unite ourselves to Him in all the good He did in this season. As the sun illuminates more of our days, we ask that these mysteries would illuminate the way that the Lord is moving in our lives through these Rosary reflections.

Opening prayer: Lord, as I enter into this new season of summer, teach me about You through these Mysteries of Light. Help me to see how You are asking me to live during ordinary time in order to unite my life to Yours. As I seek wellness and healing, reveal to me the ways that You are working to bring it about in my life. Amen.

The Baptism of Jesus

"I am baptizing you with water, for repentance, but the one who is coming after me is mightier than I.... He will baptize you with the holy Spirit and fire." (Matthew 3:11)

Jesus, You make ordinary things holy. Your baptism is the reason water became holy and has such cleansing and transformative power. It elevated baptism to the powerful sacrament that it is for us. You enable the healing waters of baptism to bring us new life. *Help us to recognize all around us that You are making ordinary things holy.*

The rite of baptism makes us want to throw off what is old and put on a new white garment. "Through Baptism the Christian is sacramentally assimilated to Jesus ... the Christian must ... go down into the water with Jesus in order to rise with him, be reborn of water and the Spirit so as to become the Father's beloved son in the Son and 'walk in newness of life'" (*CCC* 537). Allow the Lord to cleanse you and make you a new being in Him. *In what areas of your life do you long to walk in the newness of life?*

"After He was baptized, Jesus came up immediately from the water;
and behold, the heavens were opened, and he saw the Spirit of God
descending as a dove and settling on him, and behold, a voice from the
heavens said, 'This is My beloved Son, with whom I am well pleased.'"

—Matthew 3:16-17

The Wedding Feast at Cana

"Jesus told them, 'Fill the jars with water.' So they filled them to the brim. Then he told them, 'Draw some out now and take it to the headwaiter.' So they took it. And when the headwaiter tasted [it] … [he] called the bridegroom and said to him … 'you have kept the good wine until now.'" (John 2: 8-10)

Jesus, You bless our meager offerings and make them abundant. You turned jars of wine into the best and tastiest wine, flowing in abundance. The bride and bridegroom did not do anything in their own power to get this wonderful blessing, and yet You provided. *Let us never hold back our small offerings to You, hesitant that they are not substantial enough. Give us faith in Your power to transform.*

This pattern is revealed in nature all around us. Seeds that are planted and watered become flowers, veggies, and fruit. Something so small becomes a beautiful sight to behold or a yummy, nourishing snack. We plant and care for the seeds, but we are not the ones that make them grow. Let us enter into this mystery and recognize that the work of man is not all man's doing. Our efforts, united to the Lord, as small as they may seem, can lead to deep healing and improvements in health. *In what ways do you struggle to yield to the Lord's transforming grace in His time?*

The Proclamation of the Kingdom of God

"Do not store up for yourselves treasures on earth . . . But store up treasures in heaven . . . for where your treasure is, there also will your heart be." (Matthew 6:19-21)

Jesus, You came to proclaim the good news of the Lord and to bring it about here. You bring a message that is counter to what we know. Making God's Kingdom present here requires us to live in His reality rather than our own. *Reveal to me the ways that I am stuck in my own reality and that my life is not aligned with Yours, Lord. Open my eyes to my blindness and resistance.*

Living in accordance with God's reality can help set our course straight. Being rooted in His eternal truth about ourselves and our lives is so crucial as we journey through life. It gives us a clear view of what is important, recalibrating our goals and refocusing our choices. It enables us to see ourselves rightly, and this affects how we treat ourselves. As we walk this wellness journey, it is so important to remember that we want to do so in light of the Lord's kingdom — here and yet to come. *Reflect on the ways that your view of yourself or your purpose are not in line with God's view of reality. Allow this to refocus your goals.*

The Transfiguration

"Behold, a bright cloud cast a shadow over them, then from the cloud came a voice that said, "This is my beloved Son, with whom I am well pleased; listen to him." (Matthew 17:5)

Jesus, You revealed Your true glory to the disciples. The voice of God the Father revealed to them that You are who You say that You are. God wants the disciples to know who You are so they will be attentive to learning more about Him through You. *Reveal Yourself to me Lord, so I may be inspired to listen and learn more about You and grow in holiness.*

Our journey of wellness must start with a desire. We want to recognize that our desires, when rightly ordered, bring us to the Lord. He loves us and says of us, "with you I am well pleased." He is pleased with us as we are, and He gives us the grace to grow in holiness, to come to a place of health and wholeness. May our desires lead us to Him who is the source of all good things. May we never feel like we need to heal and achieve holiness before we go to Him who transforms. *Are there any wellness goals that you have not subordinated to your desire for holiness? Ask the Lord for help to begin all things from a desire for holiness and Him.*

The Institution of the Eucharist

"'Take it; this is my body' ... 'This is my blood of the covenant, which will be shed for many.'" (Mark 14:22, 24)

Jesus, You gave up Your body to redeem our souls. Your sacrifice is repeated over and over each day on the altar at Mass. Thank you for this sign of Your covenant and sacrificial love for us. You offered everything You had for us by giving up Your life, and Your being broken floods our brokenness with new life, vitality, and beauty. *Help me to enter into the mystery of Your dying to bring new life.*

The mystery of the Lord's gift of Himself for our sake resounds beyond just the altar. This reality can be seen in the daily life lived in love. As we enter into the mystery of what Jesus teaches us, we learn more deeply that love focuses on the other rather than self. It reminds us that dying to self is not for nothing, but it brings forth new life. *What are some ways you serve those you love that have become dreadful and burdensome in your mind? Ask the Lord to show you how these tasks done in love can bring growth in the life of the other.*

Closing prayer: Lord, thank You for living an ordinary life like mine so I may be inspired to live like You in each day. Make my summer season holy as I seek You above all else. Help me to live out the things that You have taught me in this time of prayer. Amen.

Sourdough Focaccia Breakfast Sandwiches

by Marisa Fredrickson

Sourdough bread can be intimidating, but focaccia is an impressive entry-level option with wonderful flavor. If you don't have sourdough starter on hand, ask around! It's likely a friend or two would love to share some with you!

Yields 8 servings.

For the Focaccia:

- 100 g active starter
- 430 g water
- 520 g all-purpose flour
- 10 g flaky sea salt
- 3 Tbsp extra virgin olive oil
- Toppings such as tomatoes, roasted garlic, and herbs

Sandwich Assembly:

- 8 eggs
- 1/2 cup cottage cheese
- Bacon, sausage, or herbs as desired

Vigorously whisk together the eggs and cottage cheese. Gently cook your eggs on the stovetop until they're just cooked through. Slice your focaccia into 8 pieces, then cut each square in half. Generously fill with scrambled eggs, and serve.

These can be kept in the fridge for a few days and then warmed in the oven at 350 degrees for 15 minutes. We often enjoy these sandwiches on Friday mornings (sans meat), though crispy bacon or sausage are welcome additions.

Instructions for the Focaccia:

1. Add water, oil, and starter to a bowl and whisk to combine. Stir in flour and salt until no dry bits remain. Let rest for 30 minutes, then perform a set of "stretch and folds" by grabbing dough from the edge of the bowl, lifting it up high, then folding it toward the center. Continue this motion 7 more times, working your way around the bowl.

2. Cover with a towel and let the dough rise at room temperature until doubled in size. In the summer this may take about 4 hours, but it is best to rely on visual cues. In the winter it could take closer to 12 hours.

3. When the dough has doubled, generously drizzle a cast iron skillet or metal pan (9x13) with olive oil. Turn the dough into the pan, fold it in thirds like a letter, and flip it over seam-side down. All sides should be covered with olive oil. Cover with a towel or wrap and place in the fridge overnight (at least 8 hours) for the second rise.

4. Preheat oven to 475 degrees. Lightly coat your fingers in a bit of oil, then using both hands, dimple the entire surface of the dough. Top with flaky sea salt, as well as tomatoes, rosemary, and roasted garlic if desired.

5. Bake for about 25 minutes, or until golden brown. Allow focaccia to cool on a rack to keep the bottom crisp. Resting in the pan will cause it to go soft.

Salt and Light

Historically, there are very few things that have been treated with as much reverence as sun and salt. It can be hard to understand since most of us grew up hearing messages of both sun and salt being bad, hence the mass production of "sun block" and "low-sodium" foods. While there seem to be more people waking up to the truth, we can't quite relate to those living two thousand years ago in how they viewed these two things.

Jesus says to His disciples: "you are the salt of the earth" and "you are the light of the world." When speaking on salt and light, Bishop Barron noted that salt "enhanced, preserved, and destroyed," while light "is a means for illumination." The relevant fact being that "they're not existing for their own sake; they exist for the sake of something else." Jesus is always intentional with His words, and this is no exception. He would not call us to be salt and light if they were not of great importance. We live in a time when Christianity is being violently opposed throughout our society, so I am not surprised that the life-giving benefits of sun and salt would also be hidden and minimized.

"You Are the Salt of the Earth"

The history of salt is ancient, and societies relied upon it heavily. Salt preserved, purified, enhanced, and improved. Civilizations prized salt for all of its uses, so much so that the Latin word for salt — *sal* — is the root for the word salary (Roman soldiers would sometimes be paid in salt). In the Catholic Church, blessed salt is a powerful sacramental (albeit a forgotten one by many). For thousands of years, people have recognized the many benefits of salt. We may not need it for food preservation today with our fancy refrigeration, but it is still essential to human life. Salt is often used interchangeably with the mineral sodium. This makes sense, as salt is made up largely of sodium chloride, though it should be noted that a good, quality sea salt will contain many more minerals alongside sodium. (For purposes of this article, I may refer to sodium as salt.)

Salt is anti-stress. Salt lowers the production of stress hormones (which is probably why we often crave it when we're stressed). When we consume too little sodium, our adrenal glands make more of the hormone aldosterone. In turn, our kidneys will conserve sodium and waste our body's potassium.

Salt is required for the function of our cells. Sodium makes up one half of our cellular pump in the body together with potassium. You can drink a few gallons of water per day and still be dehydrated if you don't consume enough salt.

Salt is important for maintaining the health of mother, baby, and placenta in pregnancy. While conventional advice today will tell women to limit sodium intake during pregnancy, many well known OB's have written extensively with an opposing opinion. Dr. Tom Brewer (and others) found that restricting salt in pregnancy led to "nearly three times more damaged placenta, two and a half times more [preeclampsia], and twice the number of infant deaths."

Salt is important for gut health. Sodium chloride is necessary for stomach acid, which, if low, has cascading effects throughout the entire body. Stomach acid protects us from pathogens, pathogenic bacteria, and parasites, while helping to keep us nourished by breaking down our food.

There are many other roles and functions of sodium. Salt increases heart rate and impacts blood pressure. It supports the nervous system by helping nerve function and the sending of impulses. It also assists in the absorption of nutrients and water in the gut.

"You Are the Light of the World"

The sun is so powerful a force that there is literally no physical life on earth without it. Sun worship was prevalent in ancient cultures; today we see idolatry of "mother nature," cloaked in pretty, abstract verbiage and/or new age practices. One of the most well-known forms of sun idolatry is ancient Egyptian worship of the sun god, "Ra."

> *And beware lest you lift up your eyes to heaven, and when you see the sun and the moon and the stars, all the host of heaven, you be drawn away and worship them and serve them, things which the Lord your God has allotted to all the peoples under the whole heaven. (Deuteronomy 4:19)*

Rather than making an idol out of the sun, we recognize it as part of God's creation on the fourth day. And despite the anti-sun propaganda that's out there today, many people intuitively know the sun is good for them. We all gravitate towards it, especially when availability has been limited (i.e.: during winter).

UVB rays are necessary to synthesize vitamin D. Contrary to popular belief, the sun does not provide vitamin D, but rather it is required for vitamin D synthesis in the skin. Other cofactors are required in this process, but sunlight is key.

Morning sunlight supports our circadian rhythms. Having morning sunlight hit our eyes (ideally not through a window) sets up a whole hormonal cascade for the day by triggering serotonin. Without enough serotonin at that time of day, we will not make enough melatonin later in the day.

Sunlight lowers blood pressure. Indoor or outdoor sunlight prompts the skin to release nitric oxide, which leads the arteries to dilate.

Sunlight and UV exposure promotes normal metabolic function. Regular exposure to morning sunlight supports hormonal function and appetite, which in turn supports normal metabolic function.

UVA & UVB rays improve skin health. Phototherapy (light therapy) has been shown to calm inflammation and reduce itching, helping with conditions like eczema, psoriasis, and other skin conditions.

The sun is an amazing good created by God. It is His will that from the sun should come so many vital means of surviving and thriving for creation. And yet just as you and I fall into the hands of our Creator, the sun is just another piece of God's dominion. The plagues in Egypt were a direct judgment on false gods, revealing the one true God. The ninth plague was a darkness over Egypt. In *Walking with God*, Gray and Cavins write, "The God who created light takes it away for three days. The God of the Hebrews blows out the sun god Re like a candle." We are reminded of Bishop Barron's words here that the sun does not exist for its own sake. And putting the sun (and salt) in its proper place, we can express our gratitude and awe for the marvelous ways God works.

Mineral Drinks

Many of us probably grew up with conventional sports drinks or hydration powders. But almost always these are full of less-than-ideal ingredients. And when ingredients tend to be far off from what the body really needs. Mineral balance is an important topic — and good to bring up practically in summertime as people are more active, sweating often, and in need of replenishment. *(Did you know that sweating, while a very good thing, depletes the body of key minerals?)*

All of these ingredients add something special to your not-so-average hydration beverage, whether it be an impressive mineral profile, a boost of vitamin C (important for adrenal health!), or other antioxidants and beneficial compounds. For instance, chlorophyll is a great source of copper, but also widely heralded as a natural deodorizer (thanks to its detoxifying effects). Instead of grabbing a cup of plain water when you're inside, try making a batch of your own hydrating drink to sip throughout the week. Here are a few examples of recipes, but feel free to get creative! *(As always, please check with your own practitioner if you have any concerns about herbals or other ingredients listed.)*

Some of our favorite mineral-rich, health-supporting teas include:

- Hibiscus
- Chamomile
- Stinging nettle
- Dandelion
- Lemon balm
- Spearmint

Below are some mineral-rich bases:

- Coconut water
- Aloe vera juice (inner fillet)

Here are some powerhouse beverage ingredients that you probably have around your kitchen:

- Pure fruit juice (orange, cherry, pineapple, etc.)
- Salt
- Lime
- Lemon
- Ginger

Special ingredients:

- Liquid chlorophyll - copper
- Mineral drops - trace minerals
- Pearl powder - calcium
- Whole food vitamin C powder
- Baobab powder - potassium

Blood Sugar Refresh

- 2 bags chamomile tea
- 12 ounces water
- 10 trace mineral drops
- Sea salt
- Honey & lemon to taste

Chamomile is known for its relaxation effects, but it is also very supportive of blood sugar balance.

Steep chamomile tea for 5-7 minutes, and mix in remaining ingredients. Pour over ice and enjoy.

Baobab Water

- 1 Tbsp baobab powder
- 1/4 tsp sea salt
- 10 oz filtered water
- Honey & lemon to taste

Baobab is rich in potassium, vitamin C, and prebiotics.

Use a frother or blender to mix the powder well with water and salt, then pour over ice. Add honey & lemon to taste.

Nettle Infusion

- 1 Tbsp dried nettle leaves
- 4 cups boiling water

Nettle is rich in many trace minerals, vitamin K, and antioxidants.

Let nettle leaves steep in water for 4-8 hours (or overnight). Strain, and then add to your beverages (or sip on its own with lemon & honey), as you'd like.

Detox Limeade

- 12 oz filtered water
- 1 dropper liquid chlorophyll
- Juice of 1 lime
- 5 fresh mint leaves
- 1/4 tsp sea salt

Chlorophyll is a great source of copper and chlorophyllins and is a great aid for detoxification.

Mix all ingredients and pour over ice.

Limeade

- 8 oz coconut water
- Juice of one lime
- 1/4 tsp sea salt

This limeade is a refreshing, summer twist on the adrenal cocktail, supplying good amounts of potassium, vitamin C, and sodium.

Mix all ingredients and pour over ice. Add magnesium bicarbonate for a bit of fizz and mineral boost.

VI

St. Michael's Lent

by Lauren DeWitt

My bare feet stick slightly to the dusty blue, peeling paint of my back porch. The incessant heat and humidity have left it somewhat tacky to the touch. A hot breath of wind — more like a petulant sigh — stirs my skirt and brings with it a cloud of mosquitoes that I swat away as I survey the yard. The grass is brown in patches. The zinnias, so bright and showy in June, now look faded. The leaves on the trees look tired. It even *sounds* hot as the cicadas strike up their tune. The dogs loll in the dirt, tongues hanging out, while my youngest child, red-faced and sweaty, begs to go to the pool. "It's closed, Love, or else I would," I reply. "Summer is over." Except that it's not. By mid-August, the world is rushing summer out the door. School is back in session, and the pools and splash pads are closed until next year. Every store loudly advertises a pumpkin spice something-or-other, and fall décor abounds, looking slightly out of place in the still-too-bright sunlight.

As for summer, herself, however; she has no intentions of leaving. Instead she lingers, lazily watching the world hurry itself on through her half-lidded eyes, like a cat snoozing in a warm patch of sunlight. She yawns at me, entirely unconcerned, as I try to guess how many more weeks until I'll sense that first, longed-for change in the air signaling autumn. There is a temptation in life to rush through the unpleasant parts, to short-circuit the suffering and distract from the boredom as much as possible. This temptation to effeminacy, slothfulness, and discontent may seem rather mild when we're talking in terms of something like waiting for the seasons to change. But a restless heart is always indicative of an underlying spiritual problem, and to ignore the more trifling symptoms is to permit room for a more serious disease to grow, to our ultimate peril.

It's easy — or at least easier — to feel "on fire" in our spiritual lives when we're in the thick of a penitential season like Advent or Lent or celebrating the joy of Christmas and Easter. Many of us are quite good at taking up new spiritual disciplines, exercising more generosity, and intentionally fasting and fighting vice during these times. Yet despite these seasons of spiritual mountain-tops, by the time the umpteenth-week in Ordinary Time after Pentecost arrives, we may find that our spiritual practices have begun to languish and wilt much like our gardens under the heat of the day-in, day-out humdrum and trials of life. It is precisely at this time of the year, however, that Mother Church invites us to look up, encouraging us to look beyond the material and to glimpse the hidden, though very active, spiritual reality surrounding us. Right around the time when the summer heat feels most oppressive, we celebrate the Solemnity of the Assumption of Our Lady on August 15th. We remember how Our Blessed Mother, upon reaching the end of her earthly life, was assumed body and soul into Heaven, where she remains even now, ceaselessly interceding for us, her children, still below. It's a reminder that ought not be missed, one that deserves a period of special consideration and prayer before we hurtle on to the next season (both calendar and liturgical).

Perhaps St. Francis of Assisi noticed a similar phenomenon in his own time because, although the medieval world he inhabited was, in some ways, more aware of unseen spiritual realities than in our own times, many churches, small shrines, and chapels dotting the countryside of Assisi lay in ruins. As St. Francis worked to rebuild the Church both physically and spiritually, he developed a great devotion to Our Lady, Queen of the Angels, and her myriad of heavenly helpers. St. Bonaventure writes in *The Life of St. Francis* that "[Francis] was joined by a chain of inseparable love to the angels.... Because of his devotion to the angels he used to fast and pray constantly during the forty days after the Assumption of the glorious Virgin. Because of the fervent zeal he had for the salvation of all, he was devoted with a special love to blessed Michael the Archangel, who has the office presenting souls to God."

This period of rigorous fasting, prayer, and almsgiving observed by St. Francis became known as St. Michael's Lent, and it was toward the end of St. Michael's Lent in 1224 A.D. that he received the stigmata. From this time up through the 18th century, St. Michael's Lent became a mid-year complement to the penitential seasons of Advent and Lent for many religious and laypersons. *The Little Flowers of St. Francis* records these words of St. Francis regarding the practice: "My sons, we are drawing nigh to our forty days' fast of St. Michael the Archangel; and I firmly believe that it is the will of God that we keep this fast in the mountain of Alvernia ... to the end that we may, through penance, merit from Christ the consolation of consecrating that blessed mountain to the honor and glory of God and of His glorious mother, the Virgin Mary, and of the holy angels." These words are for us, too. Our Lord did not speak of prayer, fasting, and almsgiving as exceptional practices in the spiritual life, ones that should take place only in limited measures at discrete times of the year. To the contrary, He *commands* us to pray without ceasing, to give without counting the cost, and to fast for the deliverance of ourselves and the world.

A contrite heart and a broken spirit transform even the most mundane parts of life into a "praise of His glory" (Ephesians 1:12). To rush headlong into the "next thing," filling our schedules with distractions and ignoring the present moment in anticipation of the supposedly greener grass on the other side, is to waste so many precious drops of His grace. Summer isn't over yet. The days are long, and it seems as though the heat will never abate. We may long for change, but let's not fail to consecrate the here and now "to the honor and glory of God and of His glorious mother, the Virgin Mary, and of the holy angels." How you choose to observe St. Michael's Lent will depend on your state in life, but community and accountability are often crucial for sustained spiritual growth. After all, the observation of St. Michael's Lent thrived in the context of the Franciscan community. Consider taking up this forty-day period as a couple if you are married, striving to add more family prayer time to your day, volunteering at a local charity together, and reducing or giving up altogether certain foods or screen time. Gather a group of women from your parish and resolve to make a Holy Hour together weekly or read a spiritual book together, checking in with one another regularly to encourage one another in whatever disciplines you choose to take up.

The ancient Desert Fathers wrote about the "noonday devil," that temptation to acedia that strikes whenever we find ourselves hungry, angry, lonely, tired, or bored — often occurring in the heat of the day. Yet St. Bonaventure, in *The Mirror of Our Lady*, writes that "[a]t the [noon hour] the sun waxeth more hot; and by means of our Lady the everlasting Sun hath shewed the heat of His charity more largely to mankind." When the summer is at its hottest and we are most tempted to discontent, we can choose to let the noonday devil win, waiting until the next big liturgical season to rededicate ourselves to prayer, fasting, and almsgiving. Or, we can imitate St. Francis in observing St. Michael's Lent, choosing instead to let the heat act as a reminder of God's love, spurring us on to show Him greater generosity and love in return.

Look up, dear sister! See our Blessed Mother smiling upon you from her heavenly throne, and see St. Michael's hand, outstretched and ready to present you to the Father, and respond to their invitation to consecrate the here and now more deeply to Our Lord.

Homegrown Cut Flowers

Words and Photos by Emily Hannon

Flowers have always been a great source of healing to me. They have comforted me in grief, bolstered me in seasons of waiting, and magnified my joy when blessings abound around me. They are a tangible reminder that God is indeed lovely and good, even in the midst of tremendous suffering. If He, the God of the Universe, has created every hue of dahlia, every petal on a peony, every delicate wisp of a cosmos — then surely He cares *even more* about me, His beloved daughter. He pursues my heart through each intricate detail and reminds me that His mercies are new every morning in the garden. Growing flowers lets me participate in the miracle of new life right alongside my Creator. It is a gift I have come to love deeply, and I believe it is a gift for everyone.

Through my garden, I must learn the virtues of patience, humility, hope, and trust as I sow seeds in the springtime and wait for them to sprout and flower all summer. It is a practice of radical hope that believes life can come from dead things and abundance from poverty. Gardening is a great act of faith, a defiance of despair. Every February, it is still an absolute miracle to me that those daffodils pop up from the cold, dark earth as if to say, "See! There is always hope!" What better way to learn and live the Resurrection than through flowers?

Although these flowers aren't feeding me as our vegetable beds do, they are just as vital. They satisfy my hunger for beauty and creativity, and they allow those parts of me to flourish. Especially as a mother to small children, I've learned that growing and arranging flowers is not just a luxury or a frivolous hobby. It truly gives life to my tired mind and reawakens the creative spark that can lay dormant when I'm overwhelmed or burnt out. The utilitarians among us will have to learn to leave room for the unexpected and mysterious and marvel at the beauty for beauty's sake, for cut flower gardens are anything but utilitarian — and thank God for that.

> "Beauty teaches us not just that God exists but that He
>
> is lovely and good. Beauty tells us that we were
>
> created for joy and summoned to healing."
>
> — Sarah Clarkson, *This Beautiful Truth*

I am still very much a beginner on my gardening journey, and every year I learn and research more ways to improve upon years past. But that is perhaps one of my favorite things about it: there is always more wisdom to gain, more knowledge and expertise to acquire. The greatest and simplest piece of advice I can offer if you are just starting out is merely to try. Buy a few packets of seeds (they're just a couple dollars each), research your growing zone and when to plant them, and then directly sow them into good soil (some flowers like cosmos actually do just fine in poor, dry soil so don't be discouraged!). As Mary from *The Secret Garden* says, all you really need is "a bit of earth … to plant seeds in — to make things grow — to see them come alive." And the joy a fresh garden bouquet picked that very morning brings me is worth every little setback or failure along the way. Over the past couple of years, I've learned some basic lessons when it comes to creating and maintaining a cut flower garden, specifically for the purpose of making homemade floral arrangements.

Choosing Flower Varieties

First, think about what flowers you love. Gather inspiration from books, blogs, magazines, or Instagram and find out what you're drawn most to. Are you envisioning neat rows of color-coordinated flowers or a wild array of cut-flower clusters wherever you can fit them? Close your eyes and let yourself dream and imagine. What do you see?

However you decide to plan out your garden, most cut flower gardens have some combination of this formula: a central focus flower, fillers, and foliage. For example, a spring or summer bouquet could include a peony or dahlia as the focus flower, snapdragons for interesting shape/height, and cosmos to soften, along with sweet peas for foliage to give everything a canvas. Be sure to choose flowers that bloom all season or take turns with others so that you always have plenty of blooms to work with.

If your cut-flower garden is not fenced in, you'll need to make sure you choose flowers that are resistant to deer and pests. I've had success growing peonies, dahlias, zinnias, sunflowers, cosmos, and snapdragons. They're all fairly easy to grow and require minimal maintenance and they're all deer resistant (cosmos and zinnias are the least fussy of them all I've found). They look lovely in beds and bouquets. My favorite places to buy seeds (besides my local nursery which sells Renee's Garden) are Johnny's Seeds and Eden Brothers (free shipping!). For dahlia tubers, I like to support my local flower farm that sells tubers every spring and then add specific varieties from dahlia farmers around the country that are harder to find. I only add two or three of these varieties every year since the cost adds up with shipping and only includes a couple of tubers per order compared to my own growing collection of tubers I've saved and divided from previous years. Some of my favorite dahlia varieties are Snoho Doris, Cafe au Lait, Cornel Bronze, Sweet Nathalie, Linda's Baby, and Ivanetti. My favorite zinnias are from the Queen Lime series and Oklahoma Salmon. I love Purity and Double Click cosmos varieties.

Planning/Prepping the Beds

First you'll need to prep your garden beds with good, well-drained soil and compost. Then measure your bed to get a general idea of how many flowers you can fit in the space. I've found that I can typically fit more flowers within a space than what the seed packets recommend. You'll want to plant the tallest flowers in the back of your bed, or wherever they won't be blocking the smaller flowers from sunlight. Since cut-flower bouquets need long, tall stems, staking or supporting them is important as they grow and bloom. Dahlias should be staked at the time of planting and then you'll tie in the branches as they grow so that they don't topple over or snap.

Designing a Color Palette

Some gardeners want a cottage-type garden with soft hues and wild, uninhibited lines. Others want formal symmetry with a specific aesthetic or color palette. Last year, I incorporated lots of rich, deep burgundies and fuschia with white and pale pink accents. This year, I'm doing primarily peaches and coral pinks. Remember, you can always experiment with different colors every year and switch things up a little! I'm focusing on cohesive hues that look lovely together in the garden, as well as in bouquets.

Harvesting Your Flowers

The best time of day to cut your flowers is in the morning and evening, since those are generally the coolest times of the day. The plants lose the most water in the heat of the day and become dehydrated, which will make them wilt faster in bouquets. Cut the stems with clean, sharp clippers and cut back the leaves that will be immersed in water. Put them directly in lukewarm water and change out the water every day. Some of my favorite vases are simply pitchers I've found secondhand at thrift stores, or a mason jar packed with a bunch of zinnias.

Decorating Your Home with Cut Flowers

I love giving bouquets to my neighbors, bringing a fresh arrangement over to a dinner party, or arranging them all over my house. There is nothing lovelier and more welcoming than a homemade bouquet on a bedside table in your guest room, or a large arrangement on your kitchen table, or a simple one on your mantle. Cut flowers instantly bring warmth and color to any home design, and I really love how they add a charm and character like nothing else can. Plus, I love that I'm greeted by a bit of my garden every morning when I walk downstairs and pour myself a cup of coffee. Don't feel pressure to create professional arrangements or buy all the fancy flower-arranging tools. Cut what appeals to you and have fun playing with the different colors and textures. I love a pitcher full of cosmos just as much as I love a lavish late-summer bouquet bursting with every flower in my garden. The feeling of seeing the fruits of your labor sprinkled throughout your home is truly the best!

FALL

Two of our primary rhythms as Catholics include the liturgical year laid out by the Church and the seasons of nature. When we realize that these two are not at odds, but are meant to be lived out in union, the order of our life can take on a new meaning. Take time this fall to contemplate what is in front of you — the colors, our gardens, the waning of days, the chill in the air — in the context of the Church. And while we practice good stewardship of our bodies, we should never do so at the neglect of our souls. These habits that can be so good are meant to serve us ultimately on our path to Heaven. Let that always be the goal — to seek first the Kingdom of God.

Fall is such an appropriate time — both liturgically and materially — to reflect on the reality of death, this consequence of sin, this truly sorrowful parting of soul and body. And yet it is appropriate to also celebrate life. So much bursts forth in the fall — some final shining moments of nature, if you will: the harvest, the bold colors, the morning and evening light. It is possible to contemplate our death and what that moment holds, while also remaining in absolute awe of life and its precious gifts. It is a delicate balance that I think we as Catholics have a unique hold on, to see both the beauty and tragedy in all these things. Fallen man in this valley of tears, but with the hope of an eternal home greater than Eden.

"Most beautiful of all was the tarnished gold of the elms,
with a little brown in it, a little bronze, a little blue,
even — a blue like amethyst, which made them melt into
the azure haze with a kind of happiness, a harmony of
mood that filled the air with content."

— Willa Cather

fall
EMBER DAYS

The September Ember Days were one of the first Ember Days instituted in the Church. This makes sense when we realize the Ember Days are so connected to our agricultural roots. They are close to the fall equinox and coincide with the general harvest season. This placement on the calendar was intentional, as the Church recognized this as an appropriate time for man to give thanks to God for all His provision in creation. Since most of us are not farmers today, it can feel like an odd practice — many of us are disconnected from the land, not as subject to the whims of nature and the elements when it comes to our means of survival. All the more reason to take these days to pause and give thanks! Whether you observe the fast or attend the liturgies or not in the transition to fall — when the created world starts to grow cold — the Ember Days provide an opportunity to praise God for His many gifts.

The autumn Embertide follows the feast of the Exaltation of the Holy Cross and the third Sunday in September. This traditionally was to give thanks for the grapes that make wine for the Precious Blood of Christ.

"Return, O Lord, a little, and be entreated in favor of
Thy servants. Lord, Thou hast been our refuge, from
generation to generation."

— The Gradual on Ember Friday

VIII
Jesus meets the
women of
Jerusalem

what's in season?
FALL

Vegetables

- Arugula
- Beets
- Broccoli
- Cabbage
- Cauliflower
- Eggplant
- Kale
- Peppers
- Carrots
- Parsnips
- Celery Root
- Potatoes
- Pumpkins
- Mushrooms
- Squash
- Sweet potatoes

Fruits

- Apples
- Cranberries
- Figs
- Pears
- Persimmons
- Grapes

Fall has perhaps the best produce associations of all the seasons. Whether you enjoy trips to a farm, specialized coffee beverages, or Thanksgiving dishes, it's not difficult to find pumpkin, squash, and apples in abundance during this time. Depending on where you live, you may still see fresh summer crops available late into the year. And while our list is not exhaustive, it's intended to be a glimpse into foods we think offer unique benefits. A little phrase to remember when it comes to plant-based carbohydrates would be "roots & fruits." Root vegetables (those that grow underground) and fresh fruit are going to be some of the most supportive carbohydrates we can consume. They are gentle on our digestion (typically cooked) and are an excellent source of energy for the body. Something to keep in mind is to always consume carbohydrates with protein and fat, to support stable blood sugar. For instance, apples cooked in butter or steamed beets topped with goat cheese.

Masala Chai

for the feast of St. Teresa of Kolkata (September 5)

by Marisa Fredrickson

Ingredients:

- 2 whole cinnamon sticks
- 1 whole star anise
- 8 cardamom pods
- 6 whole black peppercorns
- 3 whole cloves
- 3 1/4"-thick slices of ginger
- 3 Tbsp loose leaf black tea *(I use ceylon)*
- 2 1/2 cups water
- 3 cups whole or coconut milk
- Sugar or maple syrup to taste

St. Teresa spent much of her life caring for the poorest of the poor in India, treating them as if they were Jesus Himself. In honor of her feast day, consider making a comforting cup of chai, and ponder how you might be able to love and support the poor in your own community. If there are any Missionaries of Charity near you, reach out to them and ask how you can be of help!

Instructions:

1. Begin by crushing your spices in a mortar and pestle, or with a rolling pin over a cutting board. They just need to be broken down a bit, not crushed into a powder.

2. Combine spices and water in a saucepan, and bring to a boil. Once boiling, reduce the heat and simmer for 15 minutes, or until the water has reduced slightly.

3. Add the black tea and milk, cover, and steep on low heat for 10 minutes. Strain the tea and sweeten as desired. Leftovers can be kept in the fridge for 3 days.

Bringing Sacred Art Into the Home

by Megan Madden

Photos by Emily Malloy

During the latter half of my time in high school, I took a two-year humanities course where we studied some of the greatest works of art in person, from ancient times to the medieval era, all the way through the Renaissance and up to the impressionists; the whole time was spent searching out the themes and stories that surrounded each artist and their work. Wandering the Louvre in Paris, I found myself completely in awe of what surrounded me. So many of the great pieces depicted stories of the Gospels and Old Testament. They helped bring my imagination to life and make all manner of connections between the realities they depicted. They helped me to pray.

Many years later, I brought that experience into my first year of marriage, when my husband and I decided we should purchase some classical sacred art prints to hang on our walls. At the time, we were in graduate school and could not afford much, but we were able to acquire prints of works by artists like Fra Angelico, Titian, and Tintoretto — my husband's favorite artist — that we framed and hung throughout our home. Doing so reminded us that our home was a domestic church and, even though simple, we should strive to adorn it beautifully with visuals that remind us of Heaven in our everyday. A glance at the paintings here and there helped to cultivate a certain interior disposition, serving as reminders that certainly fueled us spiritually.

In the age of quick purchases, interior design novelties, and consumerism, beauty can be associated with a sort of vanity or overindulgence. Certainly too much of anything is problematic. But as Catholics we know that the Lord uses the material world so purposefully to speak bigger and deeper things. He uses humble items like salt and oil, bread and wine to bring forth spiritual riches within the sacraments. The bread and wine turn into the very Body and Blood of Our Lord, assuring us that our bodies too, are made good. When rightly ordered, the material world is here to serve us and bring us joy. Beauty (in particular) is for every person, because God deemed it so. He did so when He created the sunset and sunrise, the stars sparkling across the sky, the birds chirping, and the seeds that grow into colorful flowers that we cut and set in a vase simply to look at and enjoy. Why? Because they are beautiful. These things are free for all people to enjoy, no matter one's economic status or background.

In the same sense, God gives each of us an imagination and creative gifts that we see displayed in great pieces of literature, musical compositions, and masterful works of art. We were made to create in imitation of the Creator. We were made to foster beauty in imitation of Beauty Himself. This good and holy desire for beauty is quite simply a desire for God, to bring Him into our spaces and places (whether we know it or not). Nowhere is this more true than within our homes. Very particularly when we bring in what is transcendent and sacred, beautiful and holy.

In my own home I began bringing in sacred art pieces through simple prints, and then over time was able to thrift used and found items like statues, original paintings, and even some newer pieces from contemporary artists. Sacred art does not simply help us to pray. It gives us comfort when times are difficult. It reminds us to think of Heaven and the bigger picture of everyday life. It even acts as witness to the faith to anyone who enters our home. Fra Angelico famously painted his work for the monks with whom he lived in order to cultivate their habit of meditation. That is what sacred art does for us (and any children we may have running about as well!).

One of the ways I like to help my children in this regard is to hang artwork at their eye level. I use a piece of glossy paper, pick a painting, print it out (or cut it out of an old book), and hang it with an inexpensive frame (usually thrifted). With toddlers who may be a little more rough and tumble, I've been able to frame these pieces with plastic, or even no glass at all. This effort has brought about many deep conversations and opportunities for catechesis in our home. We can talk about the artist and the time period it came from; the children make up stories about what is happening and copy it in their own artwork, and if it depicts a Gospel story, I read about it directly from Scripture. I can ask questions like: Where is Christ in this picture? What colors do you see? How does this make you feel? All these are fruitful ways of engaging children. I've found that they have taught me so much and often see minute details in any given painting that I do not usually pick up on.

This process has been most beneficial with sacred classical art, but there are also even more traditions we can lean into! For instance, we can enthrone the Sacred Heart and Immaculate Heart of Mary images in our home, or create a home altar where the family comes together to pray with a crucifix, a candle, and spiritual books. Finding a statue of Our Lord and clothing it with the proper liturgical colors for the season is another helpful practice, as is having a liturgical calendar with which the children can engage and learn all the feast days. These are all little — but impactful — ways to foster our domestic church and pass on the faith through sacred art. Every room can have something to remind us, even if it is a small crucifix hanging above the door or prayer cards on a side table. This imagery brings peace, soothes the soul, points to the eternal, and acts as sacramentals in our daily life. It is a silent witness to the faith that helps us transcend the everyday moments, and speaks to our beliefs when others enter our home.

Years ago I stood in a crowded art museum in Paris in awe and wonder. I felt changed by the beauty I witnessed. I wanted more. Now, I've found contentment in an intentional domestic church, bringing inside life-giving pieces that speak and radiate Truth, Beauty, and Goodness that speak to the whole family. Never underestimate the power of a beautiful piece of sacred art.

St. Hildegard von Bingen

After more than 800 years had passed since she walked the lush green hills of the Rhineland in Germany, this holy woman was formally declared a saint in May of 2012 under the papacy of Pope Benedict XVI. Joining the company of our friends, Sts. Thérèse of Lisieux, Teresa of Ávila, and Catherine of Siena, Hildegard is one of only four women in history to hold the title "Doctor of the Church." St. Hildegard was described by St. John Paul II as a "light for her people and her time." Despite the centuries of change in culture, her strong, simple witness of a Benedictine life of balance and virtue still holds relevance to our modern lives. Hildegard held many titles: abbess, artist, composer, naturalist, poet, visionary, botanist, exorcist, healer, traveling preacher, and mystic, among others. She was a true model of feminine strength. She stood steadfast and true to the Lord with great respect for His creation, used her gifts well, and stayed obedient to Church authority, but was also unafraid to raise her voice to speak up and confront injustices of her time.

Born to a noble family in the year 1098, she was the tenth child in her family and thus destined for religious life from birth. During those times in Medieval Europe the tenth child was seen as the family's tithe to God. From the age of three she began to experience visions, the first of which she described as "an immense light which shook my soul." Hildegard was plagued with chronic illness most of her life, and her symptoms suggest that these visions were received during bouts of extremely intense migraines. These experiences were not apparitions or dreams, but happened when she was fully awake. On one of her most notable visions she wrote, "Heaven was opened and a fiery light of exceeding brilliance" came and commanded her to tell and write about the Lord's marvels.

Hildegard was a beautiful model of turning weaknesses into strengths for the greater glory of the Lord. Her days were rooted in the balance of prayer and work, with an emphasis on the holiness of the ordinary. She saw all of creation as a reflection of the Creator, and to her the human body was a garden to be tended to by the holy gardener Himself. One of Hildegard's biographers wrote that to her, "the physical world too has its own liturgy."

"O, You who are ever giving to all life, moving all creatures, root of all things, washing them clean, wiping out their mistakes, healing their wounds, You are our true life, luminous, wonderful, awakening the heart from its ancient sleep."

— St. Hildegard

Viriditas is a concept central to St. Hildegard's life and teachings. She describes this "greening" force as the living light that expresses God's vitality and goodness on earth. We find this first in the Garden of Eden, and we have pieces of this divine love sprinkled throughout our days, as an opportunity for wonder and for healing body and soul. She wrote, "Glance at the sun. See the moon and the stars. Gaze at the beauty of earth's greetings. Now, think. What delight God gives to humankind with all these things." Hildegard honored this connection to creation and the harmony and vitality it brings when we are living in connection with it. This holy balance was key to health and wholeness in Hildegard's eyes. The height of *viriditas* to Hildegard are flowers. Blossoms symbolizing new life to come, to her, were models of our Lord sacrificed for us, for the sake of eternal love and abundance.

Along with a deep honor for creation, Hildegard found music to be a bridge to the divine. She said, "When we sing, we repossess some of the Eden that we lost when Adam fell…. Music stirs our hearts and engages our souls in ways we can't describe." With no formal training, she left one of the largest repertoires of any medieval composer, a collection of soaring melodies that celebrate the wonders of the holy and the natural world.

With her spirit rooted in this wonder, Hildegard handled many hardships with grace. She perceived her twelfth-century church as very lukewarm, with clergy that embraced lavish lifestyles and neglected to faithfully teach the Scriptures, corruption in the Vatican, and popular religions popping up and leading the shepherd's flock astray. Even amidst health struggles and the duties of running her own abbey, she was a well-known traveling speaker of her time. Within her community, she fostered the charisms of St. Benedict and cared for the well-being of her sisters. Outside the walls of the cloister, her writings influenced many and she preached about improved discipline and practice among the faithful.

She said she struggled every day with anxiety, but never let that distract her from the deep love of her Creator. She knew beauty well, and she stayed rooted there singing praises while carrying out her witness as a disciple of her loving Father with humility and strength. When speaking about her place as a Doctor of the Church, Pope Benedict XVI said, "Her ability to speak to those who were far from the faith and from the Church make Hildegard a credible witness of the new evangelization." St. Hildegard of Bingen was a beautiful example of strength and virtue in the face of worldly troubles, a humble and joyful voice that wasn't afraid to speak words of light into what seemed to be a dark world. Her life can teach us many things, but above all, that a strongly-rooted love for the Creator has the power to spread His healing, hope, and love. We celebrate her feast day on September 17th.

A Michaelmas Feast

by Courtney Cantu

On September 29th, we celebrate the feast day of St. Michael. This feast day is rich in tradition that dates back to the fifth century. Michaelmas (pronounced Mickel-mas) is a feast day celebrating the Archangels St. Michael, St. Gabriel, and St. Raphael. St. Michael fought Satan and the fallen angels; he defends us in our battles, protects us against evil, and helps bring us out of darkness and back to the Light. Traditionally, the feast day of Michaelmas marks the end of harvest. To celebrate, families spend time picking blackberries and flowers for St. Michael. They sing, dance, and do good deeds like the angels, like going to Mass, and feasting in communion. Families feast on herbed poultry, potatoes, and vegetables to commend the new bounty of the harvest. Blackberries are picked before the end of the day because it is said when St. Michael defeated Satan, he fell into a bush of blackberries spitting and cursing, making them sour. Michaelmas memorializes the angels and their holy courage to transform darkness to light, cold to warmth, and the victory of joy we hold in our hearts as goodness reigns over evil. St. Michael embodies the defeat of darkness, and as we transition seasons we are reminded of the light that remains constant.

Each of these recipes is created to serve four people. Feel free to halve, double, or triple as needed to accommodate your guest count.

Stuffed Mushrooms

- 10 baby bella mushrooms
- 1/4 cup coconut aminos
- 2 Tbsp ghee
- 1 tsp apple cider vinegar
- 3 cloves garlic, minced
- 1 Tbsp ghee, melted
- 1/3 cup fresh parsley, chopped
- 3/4 cup gluten-free panko
- 1/4 cup nutritional yeast
- 1/2 tsp onion powder
- 1/2 tsp red chili flakes
- 1/2 tsp salt
- 1/2 tsp black pepper

Preheat the oven to 400 degrees. Gently wash the mushrooms with a damp cloth and remove stems. In a medium bowl, stir together the coco aminos, ghee, and apple cider vinegar. Add the mushrooms until covered and set aside to marinate for about 15 minutes. In the meantime, in a medium bowl combine the garlic, ghee, parsley, panko, nutritional yeast, and seasonings. Line a baking sheet with the marinated mushrooms, placing mushrooms top down. Spoon about 1-2 Tbsp of the mixture into each mushroom. *(Optional: Set aside any extra of the mixture to garnish potatoes later.)* Bake mushrooms for 10-12 minutes.

Herb Roasted Chicken

- One 4.5 lb whole organic chicken
- 2 tsp kosher salt
- 2 tsp black pepper
- 1 handful fresh parsley sprigs
- 1/4 cup fresh thyme sprigs
- 2-3 fresh rosemary sprigs
- 1 lemon, quartered
- 1 onion - one half quartered, one half thinly sliced
- 8 garlic cloves
- 1/4 cup ghee

Garlic Roasted Potatoes

- 2 lbs fingerling potatoes
- 2 Tbsp ghee
- 3 cloves garlic, minced
- 2 tsp salt
- 2 tsp pepper
- 1 fresh rosemary sprig

Preheat the oven to 400 degrees. In a large bowl, toss potatoes in ghee, garlic, salt, pepper, and rosemary. Thinly coat a large baking sheet with oil and arrange potatoes without overlapping. Bake for 15 minutes, then stir. Bake for an additional 15 minutes or until potatoes are golden and tender.

1. Preheat the oven to 400 degrees. Rinse the chicken and pat dry with paper towels. Remove the giblets from the chicken if it is not pre-done. Sprinkle 1 tsp salt and 1 tsp pepper into the chicken cavity. Stuff the chicken with fresh parsley, thyme, rosemary, lemon quarters, onion quarters, and 4 cloves garlic.

2. Tie the chicken together. Start with the cooking twine under the base of the chicken. Wrap one side of the twine around one leg a few times, then wrap the other side. Cross the two ends and pull the legs tight. Wrap the two ends around the breast, under the wings, and knot together.

3. Place the thinly sliced onions and remaining garlic cloves on the bottom of the roasting dish. Place the chicken on top. Coat the chicken in ghee, salt, and pepper on all sides.

4. Place the chicken on its side and bake for 15 minutes. After 15 minutes flip the chicken to the other side and bake for 15 minutes. Finally, place the chicken breast up and cook for an additional 35-40 minutes, or until the outside is browned and the internal temperature is 165 degrees.

5. Remove the chicken from the oven and baste with the juices, onions, and garlic. After it rests for about 7-8 minutes, cut to serve.

Blackberry Bundt

for Michaelmas (September 29)

by Marisa Fredrickson

Ingredients:

- 1 cup salted butter
- 1/3 cup cocoa powder
- 1 cup water
- 2 cups flour*
- 1 1/2 cups sugar
- 1 1/2 tsp baking soda
- 2 eggs
- 1/2 cup greek yogurt
or sour cream
- 2 tsp vanilla extract
- 2 cups blackberries

**To make this gluten-free, use 1 1/2 cups GF flour blend and 1/2 cup almond flour.*

There is a legend in many cultures that says that when satan was cast down from Heaven, he bounced onto the floor of hell and landed in a blackberry bush. Upon falling into the thorny brambles, he became so angry that he scorched them with his fiery breath. He cursed and spat on the blackberries, making them bitter. This is why the legend tells us that blackberries not harvested on or before Michaelmas are not good to eat.

Instructions:

1. Preheat oven to 350 degrees. Grease a 10- or 12-cup bundt pan with butter or coconut oil (a paper towel or clean rag is helpful for getting in nooks and crannies). Dusting the greased pan with a bit of cocoa powder will ensure a clean release after baking. Flour can also be used, but may affect the coloring of the bundt.

2. In a saucepan over medium heat, combine butter, water, and cocoa powder. Stir occasionally until butter is completely melted, then set aside.

3. In a stand mixer or large bowl, whisk together the flour, sugar, and baking soda. Slowly add the melted butter mixture and whisk until just combined, then whisk in the eggs and greek yogurt, mixing until smooth.

4. If your blackberries are large, roughly chop them so that each slice of cake will have berries throughout. No need to be precise!

5. Pour half of the batter into your prepared bundt pan, top with half of the blackberries, then add the rest of the batter and blackberries on top (they will sink when baking).

6. Bake the bundt for about 40 minutes, or until a toothpick comes out with few crumbs. Allow to cool for 15 minutes before turning it over. Brush the cake with blackberry syrup, just enough to cover the cake. If you don't have a pastry brush, spooning the syrup will work fine. While the cake is finishing cooling, prepare your ganache.

Blackberry Syrup:

- 3/4 cup water
- 3/4 cup sugar
- 1 cup blackberries

Combine all ingredients in a saucepan over medium heat. As the sugar melts, the berries will begin to soften. Bring to a simmer, mashing berries and stirring occasionally for 8 minutes. Strain out the berry fragments, and set the syrup aside. Discarded berries can be added to oatmeal or yogurt, and any extra syrup is lovely stirred into tea or sparkling water.

Ganache:

- 1 cup semi-sweet chocolate chips, or chopped chocolate.
- 1 cup heavy whipping cream or coconut cream

Warm cream in a saucepan until it has just begun to steam, but don't let it simmer. Remove from heat, add in the chocolate, and let it rest for 5 minutes before stirring until smooth. Let the ganache rest for another 10 minutes, then drizzle over your bundt cake. The longer the ganache rests, the thicker it will become. Keep this in mind when covering your bundt, as ganache that has not rested for long may run off the edges. Leftover ganache can be stirred into hot milk for hot chocolate, or poured over various other treats!

Frangipane Tarts

for Transitus of St. Francis (October 3)

by Marisa Fredrickson

The story goes that although St. Francis fasted most of his religious life, he requested one of his favorite foods (frangipane) on his death bed, brought to him by a dear friend.

Pastry Crust Ingredients:

- 8 Tbsp salted butter, softened
- 1/2 cup granulated sugar
- 1 cup almond flour
- 3 eggs, room temperature
- 1 Tbsp all-purpose or gluten-free flour
- 1 tsp vanilla extract
- 1/2 tsp cardamom (optional)

Crust Instructions:

Beat together butter and sugar until it has become light and fluffy, then beat in eggs and vanilla. Add in flours and cardamom, and beat until just combined. Frangipane can be made and stored in the fridge several days in advance.

Frangipane Ingredients:

- 1 3/4 cups flour (substitute gluten-free if needed)
- 8 Tbsp cold salted butter, cut into cubes
- 1 tsp cane sugar
- 1 egg yolk
- 1/2 cup cold water

Frangipane Instructions:

1. Combine flour and sugar in a bowl, then add the butter and stir with a fork to coat each piece. Squish each cube of butter between your fingers until each piece has been flattened.

2. Create a "well" in the center of your bowl. Whisk together the egg yolk and water in the well, then stir to combine with the dry ingredients.

3. Knead the dough gently, and add more cold water by the 1/2 teaspoon if any large dry patches remain. Form the dough into a round and wrap in plastic, pressing the dough into a disc, as this will make rolling out easier. Refrigerate 2 hours, or up to a few days.

4. Remove dough from fridge and let rest for about 15 minutes, so it can be easily rolled. Dust both sides of dough with flour, and roll out between two sheets of parchment paper until it is roughly 1/4" thick. For smaller tarts, cut circles out that are slightly larger than the tart pans and press into place, trimming any excess as needed. For a single tart, rolling the dough back around a rolling pin, then unrolling over the tart pan will make transferring easier.

5. Prick the base of your tart(s) several times with a fork, then refrigerate for 15 minutes to allow the butter to firm back up. At this time, your oven can be preheated to 375 degrees.

6. Before filling the tarts with frangipane, you will "blind bake" the pastry crust to prevent the bottoms from becoming soggy. Cut a sheet of parchment the size of your tart pan, and crumple it in your hands. Crumpling will help the paper to soften into the edges more gracefully. Place unfolded parchment over your chilled tart, fill with dried beans or rice, and bake for 15 minutes. After the initial bake, remove parchment and dried beans, and bake for 5 minutes more.

7. At this point, frangipane can be spooned into the baked tart shell(s) and baked as is, or topped with lovely seasonal stone fruit, apples, or pears. A single tart will bake for about 40 minutes, and small tarts closer to 20. When the frangipane has risen quite a bit and just started to become golden, it is done baking. Baked tarts can be topped with powdered sugar and sliced almonds, if desired.

MYERS
BAILLON
LIEBERMAN

Honoring the Dead

Praying for the dead is a spiritual work of mercy — and encouraged all year round. But in November, the Church honors the departed faithful in a particular way and invites us to do the same. Following the solemnity of All Saints Day on November 1st, where we celebrate all the saints in Heaven, comes All Souls Day on November 2nd. While perhaps a bit more sobering of a feast day than All Saints, it is a treasure on our liturgical calendar. On November 1st, we celebrate those who have finished the race and are enjoying the beatific vision. They need no prayers, but we petition them to intercede for us pilgrims below. On November 2nd, we remember and honor the dead who left this life in friendship with Christ but are undergoing purifications before entering Heaven. Just as with the saints, we can — and should — ask those in Purgatory to pray for us. But unlike the saints, they still need our prayers, as they have yet to reach Heaven and are unable to pray for themselves.

The feast of All Souls is such a powerful reminder of our mortality, of the reality of sin and its effects, to pray for those suffering souls, and to do all we can to avoid sin ourselves so as to limit or avoid our own time in Purgatory. St. Catherine of Siena once said, "I do not think that apart from the felicity of Heaven, there can be a joy comparable to that experienced by the souls in Purgatory" and yet "they endure pain so intense, that no tongue is able to describe it." This is a hard truth for our human minds to comprehend, and yet we take it on faith that while Purgatory is a pure gift from the Father (for so few of us leave this life perfect), it also entails immense suffering. We should all be striving to avoid sin and aspire to the heights of holiness; praise God that we have the chance to do this as long as we live. As soon as we die, though, we lose the ability to gain merit for ourselves. The holy souls in Purgatory, therefore, are in desperate need of our prayers.

"Eternal Father, I offer Thee the Most Precious Blood of Thy Divine Son,
Jesus, in union with the Masses said throughout the world today, for all the
holy souls in purgatory, for sinners everywhere, for sinners in the universal
Church, those in my own home and within my family. Amen."

— Prayer of St. Gertrude

By our prayers and sacrifices, we can help speed up their entrance into Heaven. The Church lays this out clearly in the *Catechism* (958): "'In full consciousness of this communion of the whole Mystical Body of Jesus Christ, the Church in its pilgrim members, from the very earliest days of the Christian religion, has honored with great respect the memory of the dead; and 'because it is a holy and a wholesome thought to pray for the dead that they may be loosed from their sins' she offers her suffrages for them.' Our prayer for them is capable not only of helping them, but also of making their intercession for us effective."

That final part is a beautiful piece to reflect on: "Our prayer for them is capable not only of helping them, but also of making their intercession for us effective." St. Alphonsus Maria de Liguori, Bishop and Doctor of the Church, wrote, "By assisting them we shall not only give great pleasure to God, but will acquire also great merit for ourselves. And, in return for our suffrages, these blessed souls will not neglect to obtain for us many graces from God, but particularly the grace of eternal life. I hold for certain that a soul delivered from Purgatory by the suffrages of a Christian, when she enters paradise, will not fail to say to God: 'Lord, do not suffer to be lost that person who has liberated me from the prison of Purgatory, and has brought me to the enjoyment of Thy glory sooner than I have deserved.'"

Consider that thought for a moment: those we pray for may be the ones who most fervently petition God for our salvation. As Venerable Fulton Sheen said, "As we enter Heaven, we will see them, so many of them, coming towards us and thanking us. We will ask who they are, and they will say 'a poor soul you prayed for in purgatory.'" The practice of praying for the dead, and having Masses offered for the dead, is one largely continued by those faithful little old ladies and often forgotten by the young. Of course, life gets busy and we have so many commitments and disciplines to attend to. But honoring and praying for the dead is a devotion that is for all of us. We will all leave this life, and if our life has led us to Purgatory, we will likely be hoping with our entire being that someone on earth will have the charity to pray for us that we might be released from its pains. It is also a practice that contributes to our own sanctity, storing up treasure in Heaven. St. Alphonsus Maria de Liguori tells us,

> *The practice of recommending to God the souls in Purgatory, that He may mitigate the great pains which they suffer, and that He may soon bring them to His glory, is most pleasing to the Lord and most profitable to us. For these blessed souls are His eternal spouses, and most grateful are they to those who obtain their deliverance from prison, or even a mitigation of their torments. When, therefore, they arrive in Heaven, they will be sure to remember all who have prayed for them.*

This November, let us carve out time and space for this devotion. Let us practice it faithfully and may it become a part of our daily life. *Eternal rest grant to them, O Lord, and let perpetual light shine upon them. May the souls of the faithful departed, through the mercy of God, rest in peace. Amen.*

Soul Cakes

for the feast of All Souls (*November 2*)

by Marisa Fredrickson

Yields about 16 cakes.

Ingredients:

- 7 Tbsp softened butter
- 1/2 cup cane or coconut sugar
- 2 egg yolks
- 1 1/2 cups all-purpose or gluten-free flour
- 1 tsp mixed spice, or pumpkin pie spice (feel free to get creative with baking spices you have)
- 2 Tbsp milk
- 1/3 cup raisins, or dried fruit of your choice

Instructions:

1. Preheat oven to 350 degrees. Beat together butter and sugar until well combined. Add the egg yolks one at a time, and then the flour and spices, mixing until it just comes together. Stir in the dried fruit with a spoon or by hand, then transfer the dough to a floured surface.

2. Roll out the dough to be about 1/2" thick, and cut into rounds using a biscuit or cookie cutter. Using a sharp knife, mark the tops of your cakes with a cross. Place on a parchment-lined baking sheet and bake for 20-25 minutes. A dusting of powdered sugar is optional, but delicious.

The Old English and Irish custom of "souling" or "soul-caking" is thought to be the origin of modern-day trick-or-treating. On All Souls Day, children would go around the town singing songs and praying, while stopping at homes to beg for a "soul cake" in remembrance of the dead. Each cake eaten was thought to represent a soul being freed from Purgatory. These cakes taste like a lovely combination of scone and cookie and are wonderful with a cup of hot tea or cider. Traditionally they are made with British "mixed spice," but pumpkin pie spice will work just fine.

Sourdough Rose Buns

for the feast of St. Elizabeth (*November 17*)

by Marisa Fredrickson

Bun Dough Ingredients:

- 8 Tbsp (113 g) salted butter, melted
- 3/4 cup (184 g) whole milk
- 1 large egg
- 1/2 cup (100 g) sourdough starter*
- 2 Tbsp (24 g) sugar
- 3 cups (360 g) flour

**If you don't have access to sourdough starter, you can swap the dough for your favorite cinnamon roll dough.*

Cardamom Filling Ingredients:

- 5 Tbsp salted butter, softened
- 1/3 cup brown sugar
- 1 1/2 tsp ground cardamom

Cardamom Glaze Ingredients:

- 1/4 cup water
- 1/4 cup brown sugar
- 1/2 tsp vanilla
- 1/2 tsp ground cardamom
- 1 tsp organic rose petals, plus more for decorating (optional)

St. Elizabeth was known for her remarkable generosity and compassion toward the poor and would often deliver bread to the hungry. Her husband, Ludwig, supported and encouraged her endeavors. One day as Elizabeth was carrying bread to share, she encountered her husband and his hunting party. To show his companions that she was not stealing from the castle's treasury, Ludwig asked her to reveal what was hidden in her cloak. Elizabeth's cloak fell open, revealing many white and red roses in place of bread. While Ludwig's companions may have been astonished, he saw this as a sign that his wife's actions were pleasing to God. These rose-shaped buns are a delicious reminder of "The Miracle of the Roses" and the virtue of generosity. This recipe makes about 10 buns, though I love to double it and share them!

Instructions for the Dough:

1. In a small saucepan, melt the butter, then turn off the heat and add the milk. Allow it to cool slightly before proceeding. We don't want the mixture too hot.

2. In the bowl of a stand mixer fitted with a paddle attachment, combine the egg, sourdough starter, and sugar. While mixing on low, slowly pour in the milk and butter. Add in the flour and continue mixing until a sticky dough forms. Scrape the sides of the bowl, cover with a damp towel, and let rest for 30 minutes.

3, Switch to the hook attachment, and knead the dough on medium speed for 8 minutes. If the dough seems sticky, add 1 Tbsp more flour. It should be soft and smooth and pull away from the sides of the bowl. When you stretch a bit of the dough, you should be able to nearly see through it (this is called the "windowpane test"). Mix a bit longer if needed.

4. Coat your bowl with a bit of butter and place the dough back inside to rest overnight, or until doubled. This should take around 8 hours, depending on how warm your home is. If you are concerned about it becoming over-proofed, simply pop the bowl in your fridge to slow fermentation.

Bun Assembly Instructions:

1. Roll out your dough on lightly floured parchment. Aim to make a rectangle that is 13x20 inches. If you find your edges are misshapen, fold them in, then keep rolling.

2. Mix all of your filling ingredients together, then spread it across the surface of the dough with a spatula.

3. Fold the right third of the dough toward the center, then the left, like you're folding a letter. Roll out the dough slightly again so that it is an even thickness.

4. With the long side of the dough facing you, cut 1 1/2" strips down its length.

5. To form your roses, twist 2 strips of dough together, then roll them up into a round. Tuck each bun into a lightly oiled cupcake pan, allowing the "tail" to go in first and fill the bottom of each cup. Allow the buns to rest and rise for one hour.*

6. Preheat your oven to 350 degrees. Prepare your glaze by combining all of the ingredients in a saucepan over medium heat, stirring regularly. Bring it to a simmer, then turn it off.

7. When the buns have risen, place them in the oven and bake until they are golden brown, about 25 minutes.

8. Immediately after removing the buns from the oven, brush them with the glaze and top with more crushed rose petals. It's important not to wait long to glaze them. Allow the buns to cool slightly before removing them from the pan, but not so long that they stick. These are best served fresh, but will keep for 2 days.

Instead of letting them rise, you can freeze the buns in the pan, and then let them thaw in the fridge before rising and baking at a later time.

Tips for a Nourishing Thanksgiving

Quality over quantity. You don't need 14 sides and 10 desserts to impress everyone. Having fewer options, but making them nutrient-dense and delicious will go a lot farther around the dinner table.

Roots & fruits. Thanksgiving is the perfect holiday to really embrace those root veggies and fall fruits. While it can be tempting to make a lot of the dishes grain-heavy, let the table reflect your desire to truly nourish those around it. For many people, root vegetables are easier to digest than things like kale, brussels sprouts, or cauliflower. While cruciferous veggies may make up some of your favorite side dishes, just try to round it out with things like beets, potatoes, carrots, or squashes. While it is common to include fruit with the desserts, we also encourage having fruit with the main course! Fruit contains fructose, which requires little to no insulin to get into the cell. When paired with a carbohydrate like a potato, the fructose helps slow down the glucose, which allows for a slower rise in blood sugar.

If possible, aim for homemade. Of course, there are many factors at play, and some people simply prefer canned cranberries or yams. But if you can, opt to make them yourself! Homemade cranberry sauce is quite simple and so tasty. And if you have a starter going, we all know fresh sourdough is a crowd favorite.

Less is more. There are many fancy recipes out there, but so many of these foods need very little to win hearts. Seasoning doesn't need to be over the top, as quality sea salt enhances everything and a few herbs can have a big impact. Homemade whipped cream for your stewed fruits, butter for your potatoes, a little bit of natural sweetener with the squash, some cider with your turkey. Think of our ingredients as highlighting or enhancing the whole food, not masking it.

> "And let the peace of Christ control your hearts, the peace into which you were also called in one body. And be thankful. Let the word of Christ dwell in you richly, as in all wisdom you teach and admonish one another, singing psalms, hymns, and spiritual songs with gratitude in your hearts to God. And whatever you do, in word or in deed, do everything in the name of the Lord Jesus, giving thanks to God the Father through him."
>
> — Colossians 3:15-17

The Art of Walking

We've lost the art of walking as a culture. With cars, buses, trains, bikes, even electric scooters, it's not something that people really take the time for. It's not the quickest way to get from point A to B, but sometimes it's the act of slowing down that confers the most meaning. With moderate temperatures and bursting colors, there is hardly a better time to pick up the habit of the after-dinner walk, also known as the constitutional. Whether your meal is with your spouse, children, parents, roommates, friends, or whoever, suggesting a golden-hour walk post-dinner is the perfect way to cultivate more depth to your relationships while supporting your health in the process.

Dinner tends to be most people's heaviest meal. That's not a criticism, but dinner is often a time to sit down together and share food that has taken time to prepare. A roasted chicken, a slow-cooked bone-in cut of meat, a hearty stew — these dishes live on in our senses and memories from childhood. Following dinner, many take that time as an opportunity to relax on the couch, perhaps put on some television. It's not that this can't be a good activity, but that there may be better alternatives in many instances. Choosing to go outside, get some fresh air, expose your eyes to the sun's evening light, walking, and talking with loved ones — this is something to be cherished. This constitutional can be a time to pray a Rosary together, discuss the architecture in your neighborhood, admire gardens and landscapes, run into neighbors, express your gratitude for moments of your day, or just to simply be present to one another.

There are also the health benefits as well; walking has an immediate glucose-lowering effect following a large meal. While running can increase cortisol levels, walking is typically not a stressor, and the leg muscles will help glucose to be taken up from the bloodstream. So a fifteen-to-thirty-minute walk can also have a blood sugar stabilizing effect. Walking will also support the proper breakdown of food; the motions of your torso help gut motility. Walking is also one of the simplest ways to support our lymphatic system, which needs our help to get things circulating. This fall, let's try to embrace the postprandial walk and reap the benefits in our body and our relationships.

"Walking isn't just a period of time in which you can be checking

the exercise box; it's also checking the box on your friendships,

relationships, work, other to-do list things."

— Katy Bowman

Creative Thanksgiving Additions

by Marisa Fredrickson

While many Thanksgiving sides are quite rich, these are some options to offer a welcome lightness to your table.

AUTUMN SALAD

Ingredients:

- 4 cups kale
- 1/4 cup freshly grated parmesan
- 2 honeycrisp apples, thinly sliced
- 1/2 cup pomegranate arils
- 1/2 delicata squash, deseeded and sliced into 1/2-inch crescents
- 3 Tbsp pumpkin seeds

Instructions:

1. Roast your squash. Preheat oven to 450 degrees. Drizzle squash with your fat of choice, and season with salt and pepper and 1 Tbsp of maple syrup. Roast until browned and then set aside.

2. Place the kale in a large bowl, then drizzle a small amount of the vinaigrette over it and massage it into the kale with clean hands.

3. Add in and arrange the sliced apples, parmesan, pumpkin seeds, squash, and pomegranate. Serve with more dressing on the side. *If you are making this several hours in advance, consider letting the apples sit for a few minutes in water mixed with lemon juice to keep them from browning.*

Vinaigrette:

- 1 Tbsp maple syrup
- 2 Tbsp apple cider vinegar
- 2 Tbsp extra-virgin olive oil
- 1 tsp cinnamon
- 1 tsp dijon mustard
- Dash cayenne pepper
- Salt and pepper, to taste

Combine all of the vinaigrette ingredients in a jar with a lid. Shake to combine. Store any leftovers in the fridge for 1 week

HARVEST MOCKTAIL MULES

Ingredients:

- 1 12-oz bottle of ginger beer
- 2 limes
- 1/2 cup pear nectar
- 1 pear, sliced
- 2 cinnamon sticks
- 1/2 cup water
- 1/2 cup cane sugar
- 1 tsp ground cinnamon

Instructions:

1. Make the cinnamon syrup. In a small saucepan, combine the sugar, water, and cinnamon. Bring it to a boil, then turn off the heat and allow it to cool to room temperature. This syrup will keep for 2 weeks in the fridge and can be used to sweeten tea or coffee as well.

2. Fill 2 cups with ice. Pour 1/4 cup of pear nectar into each cup, then squeeze the juice from a whole lime on top. Add 1/2 Tbsp of cinnamon syrup, then fill the rest of the cups with ginger beer.

3. Top with a cinnamon stick and a slice of pear.

Creative Thanksgiving Additions II

KATE'S CRANBERRY APPLE STUFFING

My sister-in-law, Kate, makes her family recipe when we are together for Thanksgiving. Stuffing was something I always passed over — until trying hers! I hope you enjoy these unique flavors as much as we do.

Ingredients:

- 1 loaf egg or challah bread
- 1/2 lb butter
- 1 large white onion, chopped
- 1 cup chopped celery
- 1/4 cup dried apricots
- 2 granny smith apples, diced
- 1/2 cup golden raisins
- 1 can whole cranberry sauce
- 1/2 tsp thyme
- 1/2 tsp savory (optional)
- 2 tsp salt
- 4 large eggs, lightly beaten

Instructions:

1. Preheat oven to 325 degrees. Tear the bread into pieces and place several handfuls at a time in a food processor. Pulse until you have coarse crumbles (if you don't have a food processor, you can just tear the bread into small pieces).

2. Place crumbled bread into a shallow roasting pan (a cookie sheet works well too) and bake at 325 degrees for 30-40 minutes, stirring every 10 minutes until the bread is slightly browned.

3. Remove from the oven and increase the temperature to 350 degrees. In a medium saucepan, melt the butter. In a separate pan, sauté the onions and celery until soft.

4. Pour the onions, celery, and browned breadcrumbs evenly into a casserole dish (we like to use a 9x13).

5. In the saucepan with the melted butter, stir the apricots, apples, raisins, cranberry sauce, thyme, savory, salt, and beaten eggs together.

6. Add the stirred ingredients into the casserole dish until evenly combined with the breadcrumbs, celery, and onions. Cover with foil.

7. Bake the stuffing at 350 degrees for 25 minutes. Remove foil after 25 minutes and bake for another 15 minutes. This stuffing can be made a day in advance and reheated at 350 degrees for 30 minutes before serving.

CRISPY BRIE WITH
BROWN BUTTER

Ingredients:

- 1 8-oz wheel of brie
- 1/2 cup panko breadcrumbs (*use gluten-free panko if needed, or crushed plantain chips*)
- 1 egg, whisked
- 1 sliced pear
- 1 small handful fresh sage leaves, cut lengthwise
- 1/4 cup chopped pecans or hazelnuts
- 5 Tbsp salted butter, divided
- Honey for drizzling
- Crackers for serving

Instructions:

1. Brush the top and bottom of the brie with the
whisked egg, then dip it into the panko. Place
the brie on a plate and set it in the freezer for
15 minutes. This will help it to keep its form
when cooking.

2. Add 2 Tbsp of butter to a small pan over
medium heat. Add the brie to the pan and cook
for a few minutes on each side, allowing the
panko to become crisp and deep brown. Once
done, remove the brie and place it on a plate for
serving.

3. Add the remaining butter to the pan, swirl-
ing the butter occasionally. Once the butter has
just begun to brown, add the sage leaves, pear,
and nuts. Continue cooking until the sage has
become crisp.

4. Pour the toppings over the brie, arranging as
you see fit. Drizzle a bit of honey across the top,
and serve immediately.

Rosary Reflections for Fall

by Emily Patteson

As we enter into the fall season, we turn again to Our Lady's intercession in this second set of Rosary reflections. During this season, the leaves begin to decay and die, we remember the dead in November, and the days are slowly getting shorter. We pray the Sorrowful mysteries to unite what is physically occurring in nature around us to the death of Our Lord. In these reflections we seek to recognize the necessity of death as we reflect on all the Lord did for us in His suffering and death.

Opening prayer: Lord, as the days get shorter and colder as we enter the season of fall, please open my heart to all that You want me to understand about suffering. When I see the leaves fall and feel the pain of my own falling leaves, may I cling to You. Help me to not lose sight of how You are working but always look to You on this journey. Amen.

The Agony in the Garden

"He advanced a little and fell to the ground and prayed that if it were possible the hour might pass by him; he said, 'Abba, Father, all things are possible to you. Take this cup away from me, but not what I will but what you will.'" (Mark 14:35-36)

Jesus, You knew all of the suffering You were to undergo, and yet You surrendered Your will. You show us how to let go of our own desires for the sake of the Father's will. Even in asking for the cup to pass, You acknowledge the power and knowledge of the Father. *Help us to surrender our will to the Father's, despite the suffering we may be facing.*

Surrendering our will requires a kind of death. Our pride and ego of feeling like we know what is best for ourselves must be laid down. This may mean some dreams we have held dear for so long must finally come to rest. Just as the Lord did in the garden, we seek to resign ourselves to the will of God. *Do you have any areas of your life where you need to put your own plans to death so you can be more resigned to the will of God?*

> "But who will endure the day of his coming? And who can stand when he appears?
> For he is like the refiner's fire, or like the fuller's lye. He will sit refining and purifying silver, and he will purify the sons of Levi, refining them like gold or like silver
> that they may offer due sacrifice to the Lord."
>
> — Malachi 3:2-3

The Scourging at the Pillar

"Then he released Barabbas to them, but after he had Jesus scourged, he handed him over to be crucified." (Matthew 27:26)

Jesus, You were scourged, not for Your own sins but for ours. Each horrible blow led to a deep wound, a tearing of skin, a loss of blood. Each strike was reparation for our sins that we may be purified. As a metal is stripped of its impurities in the fire, Your suffering removed the stains of our sin with each blow You received. *We long to be purified in the fire of Your love, Lord.*

When we think of purification as a stripping of the excess, we can think of the trees as fall progresses. In order to conserve energy in the winter, they drop their leaves. If trees clung to their leaves, they would not survive. Sometimes we cling to things. The Lord wants to strip us from the unnecessary things that take us away from the more important things in our lives — the primary things. The Lord purifies us from these things for our own good. *Is there an area in your life where you must open your hands? Imagine the relief that will come from releasing your grip as you picture the heaviness of all the leaves even one tree drops. Sit with this feeling of lightness and allow this to encourage you to let go.*

The Crowning with Thorns

"They clothed him in purple and, weaving a crown of thorns, placed it on him. They began to salute him with, 'Hail, King of the Jews!' and kept striking his head with a reed and spitting upon him. They knelt before him in homage. And when they had mocked him, they stripped him of the purple cloak, dressed him in his own clothes, and led him out to crucify him." (Mark 15:17-20)

Jesus, You are the King of the Universe. Yet, these soldiers mocked You as they treated You like a king. If only they knew how wrong they were in their view of the situation. You did not need to explain or prove anything to them about who You were. Your identity alone stood for itself, true even if others did not recognize it. *Give us the courage to live out Your will and have peace in it even when others do not understand.*

What does it feel like when you think something is going to be the culmination of tough labor (a crowning) but then you end up being misunderstood, mocked, and rejected? Has this ever happened when you have chosen to seek God's will instead of the world's path of power, money, and progress? Just as Jesus did not need to explain Himself to the soldiers, we might not have the words to explain to the world what the Lord is doing. *Is there an area in your life where you feel misunderstood? Ask the Lord for the strength to persevere as He did.*

The Carrying of the Cross

"Then he handed him over to them to be crucified. So they took Jesus, and carrying the cross himself he went out to what is called the Place of the Skull, in Hebrew, Golgotha." (John 19:16-17)

Jesus, You shouldered the cross which was not Yours to bear. Despite this, You bore its weight without complaining. Even when You fell three times, You stood back up, picked up the Cross and continued on silently. *Teach us to carry our crosses without complaining and groaning about the weight we bear.*

One important thing we can learn from Christ in this mystery is to carry our crosses without complaining. When we resolve not to complain, we are able to see how the Lord is working in our hardships. We might not understand what He is doing, but we surely are not able to see the good when we are complaining. Let us imitate our Lord and all of nature by being obedient even unto death in silence. *Is there some suffering in your life that you have spent more time complaining about than praying about? Ask the Lord to silence the inner grumbling that drowns out the voice of gratitude and blinds us to His movements in our hardships.*

The Crucifixion

"When Jesus had taken the wine, he said, 'It is finished.' And bowing his head, he handed over the spirit." (John 19:30)

Jesus, You died for our sakes. By Your dying You united Yourself to us in all things. When we experience any type of death, we are unified with You, Lord. Just as You handed over Your spirit, we seek to hand over our baggage, masks, crutches for faith, and anything else that keeps us from You. *Help us to feel united to You, Lord, as we face the little deaths in each day.*

The very act of dying, stripping of excess, unites us to Christ's physical death. Additionally, when we are stripped of these things, we have more room for Christ to dwell richly in us. There are fewer things in the way of our choosing to love Him and our relationship with Him. In November, we celebrate those who have passed. As we do, we pray that they will be united with Christ and that we will follow them to His presence when our time comes. *Is there some type of "death" you are experiencing right now? Ask the Lord to comfort you with the knowledge that despite the pain, you are united to His death.*

Closing prayer: Lord, thank You for suffering for my sake so that I do not have to suffer alone. Teach me how to suffer and the meaning of my suffering. Help me to take with me all that You have put on my heart during this time so I can go forth more open to You than before. I want to be united to You as I walk through life. Amen.

How the Homemaker Can Imitate Mary's Divine Wisdom

by Mackenzie Worthing

Our Lady has long been associated with Wisdom. One of her great titles (and in my top three personal favorites) is Mary, Seat of Wisdom — referring to Jesus as the Word made Flesh, the Uncreated Wisdom of God. Mary also enjoys a special spousal relationship with the Holy Spirit, and one of the great Gifts of the Holy Spirit is Wisdom. Mary has long been identified by saints and scholars with the feminine Lady Wisdom in the Old Testament in the books of Proverbs and Sirach.

One of the ten given Marian virtues is Divine Wisdom. We might see what that means for Mary — she was given great gifts of Wisdom through the Father's bestowal of her Immaculate Conception (which means her intellect was unclouded by sin!), through her prompt response to the Holy Spirit, and through her mothering of the Word Incarnate. Her life, beginning to end and into eternity, is imbued with the Wisdom of God. How can we, homemakers, wives, mothers, and daughters, hope to imitate this virtue? How can she show us the way to cultivating Divine Wisdom in our own lives?

Let's start with some definitions: divine simply means "proceeding from God." According to *The Catholic Dictionary*, wisdom is defined as, "The first and highest gifts of the Holy Spirit. It makes the soul responsive to God in the contemplation of divine things.... Built into wisdom is the element of love, which inspires contemplative reflection on these divine mysteries, rejoices dwelling on them, and directs the mind to judge all things according to their principles." Divine Wisdom, then, is a gift of God that opens up the person to respond to God in love and to contemplate the divine mysteries. It also has a practical element of enabling that person to then make judgments and decisions according to what they understand. Wisdom consists of both interior reflection and exterior action. An action that is considered wise is the fruit of the interior contemplation and response to the Lord's gift.

Mary is the model of these twin elements of the contemplative and the active. She was a homemaker, a wife, and a mother. She had practical duties to which she had to attend. And could any other homemaker ever attend to her home and family with such care? She is the perfect woman. Everything she did, she did beautifully. Everything she did, she did with joy. How much more so because her life was not only dedicated to serving her family in the usual way, but because in her midst was the Son of God!

A beautiful portrayal of Mary's Divine Wisdom in action is given in the painting *The Holy Family with a Little Bird* by the Spanish artist, Murillo. In it, Mary is seated at her spindle and the thread is in her hand. She has a basket of laundry on the floor beside her. The center of the painting is Our Lord as a little Child, held up by St. Joseph. Jesus holds a little bird in His hand and a dog plays at His feet. Mary's hands are busy at her task but her eyes are fixed on her Divine Son. She attends to the practical necessities, but *it is not at the expense of contemplating Our Lord.* She is able to complete her menial tasks without being consumed by them. She makes the time for both the practical and the interior life. She neglects nothing.

As for me, I have much to learn from Our Lady when it comes to this particular virtue. I usually swing in one direction or the other: I am consumed by my housework and the demands of being a wife and mother, or I neglect my practical affairs for prayer. The former is usually where I land. I must work more and more diligently at finding Our Lord in my daily duties. Obviously, there must be set times for prayer throughout our day, whether it be making a morning offering, praying the Divine Office, setting aside time to read the Bible, attending an adoration hour, or assisting at Holy Mass. But Mary's life of contemplation was not only fed by set times for prayer. She sought out contemplative moments throughout her day. It might be easy to point out the fact that she did have Jesus in her home for thirty years, so all she had to do was glance His way to behold the face of God. Yet, she also had years where He was less accessible, as during His ministry, and years of her life where He had already ascended to Heaven. Do we not have Christ with us always present in our souls as long as we are in a state of grace? Are not the other people in our homes and in our lives other Christs to whom we can glance to contemplate the mysteries of God? We are called to look for Him everywhere and always, to seek Him in each moment of our lives, and to love and serve Him well.

St. Frances of Rome notably wrote, "It is most laudable in a married woman to be devout, but she must never forget that she is a housewife. And sometimes she must leave God at the altar to find Him in her housekeeping." Our hearts might long to stay in a quiet, cool chapel to converse with Our Lord, and we need to do this when we can. But the reality is that we must also seek Him in our homes — at the kitchen sink, organizing the closets, kissing scraped up knees, welcoming the man of the house home with a smile, and in finishing up the last tasks before resting for the evening. He is there. He is there in our little tasks as well as the big ones. He is there in the little children in our lives as well as the adults. Doing what we must do is not antithetical to contemplating how and why He made the world with all its variety, or thinking about the journey on which He took the Israelites thousands of years ago, or slowly meditating on the miracles of Jesus in the Gospels. These can all be done as we do our housework. The more we build contemplation into our day, the better we can fulfill the tasks entrusted to us, for the better we will be able to imitate Our Lord, Our Lady, and all the saints. The more we contemplate all of God's goodness, the deeper we are able to grow in Divine Wisdom, the better we will be able to govern ourselves and our homes according to His virtues. May we respond to the gift of God's love and contemplate His holy mysteries throughout our days, whether we be in the chapel on our knees or sweeping the floor of the kitchen. *Our Lady, Seat of Wisdom, pray for us!*

WINTER

Every year that passes is unique from the last, and yet there is a familiarity in the soul as we enter a new season. As we look forward to the good things to come, our memories seem to recall with warmth the times past. There are probably many reasons why seasons are so short. We immerse ourselves in them but can become weary by the end. While winter can be a rough season for many, it is natural this time of year to experience a gentle ache for the stillness and silence, or even the cool temperatures and snow.

God wants to pour out many graces upon you this season, though it can easily oscillate between holiday busyness and cabin fever. Winter might feel like two seasons, which makes sense because it spans four liturgical seasons — the final days of Advent, Christmas, ordinary time, and the beginnings of Lent! When you think about it, this is a lot to move through spiritually. And for many of us, we feel this very profoundly as winter begins with moderate to cool temperatures, perhaps some beautiful light coatings of snow. But as we move beyond the joy of Christmas, we are left with an extended period of extreme cold and a covered ground that struggles to emerge amidst the piling of snow.

We invite you this season to strive for presence, to be obedient to the moments of each day that God is offering to you. And if the season feels too heavy, cling to the rhythm of the Church as your companion. We hope that it is a beautiful one for you.

"For as the rain and the snow come down from
heaven, and return not thither but water the earth,
making it bring forth and sprout, giving seed to the
sower and bread to the eater, so shall my word be
that goes forth from my mouth; it shall not return to
me empty, but it shall accomplish that which I purpose, and prosper in the thing for which I sent it."

— Isaiah 55:10-11

winter
EMBER DAYS

"Unhappily, our hearts are not sufficiently pure and free from all earthly affections. If you take a very clean and very dry sponge, and soak it in water, it will be filled to overflowing; but if it is not dry and clean, it will take up nothing. In like manner, when the heart is not free and disengaged from the things of the earth, it is in vain that we steep it in prayer; it will absorb nothing."

—St. John Vianney

Advent is technically a penitential season, although practiced in a very different way than Lent. While most of us know it's a time to clean house interiorly before the wonderful feast of Christmas, the festivities around us can often overwhelm our good dispositions. Enter in the winter Ember Days — a built-in three days on the calendar to bring our minds and hearts back to God. While not required in the U.S. since the 1960s, we can still participate ourselves and make the practice more known. Situated in the third week of Advent, an intentional fast can reorient our spirits towards the true anticipation of Christ's incarnation.

The winter Embertide follows the feast of St. Lucy. This traditionally was to give thanks for the olives that make holy oils for Unction.

"Drop down dew, ye heavens, from above, and let the clouds rain just:
let the earth be opened, and bud forth a Savior."

—Introit of Ember Wednesday

what's in season?
WINTER

Vegetables

- Beets
- Cabbage
- Carrots
- Celeriac
- Fennel
- Kohlrabies
- Leeks
- Parsnips
- Potatoes
- Rutabagas
- Shallots
- Turnips
- Winter squash

Fruits

- Clementines
- Grapefruits
- Kiwis
- Kumquats
- Lemons
- Oranges
- Persimmons
- Pomegranates
- Tangerines

For many of us, what we can find fresh and local during the winter months is limited. Potatoes and carrots may abound, but how do we add in more color, flavonoids, and minerals? First, let's step back and think about our ancestors. To be clear, we are different than our ancestors, so we don't necessarily want to eat exactly as they did for a number of reasons. Still, physiologically, we have not really evolved that much. And so taking into account the way our environment and lifestyles have changed, and therefore how they impact us as humans, is a better approach. That said, seasonal eating is something humans have been doing for thousands of years, and this is essentially because it was all that was available to them. It's especially easy in the winter to just prioritize pantry staples while grocery shopping, since quality (affordable) produce can sometimes be scarce, but prioritizing seasonal fruits and vegetables can help with both. Wherever you can, add more color! Diversity and nutrient density are key. Also important to note is that when fresh fruit is not available, frozen fruit is a great option. It is typically harvested at peak ripeness and then flash frozen on-site. This means it retains most of its nutrients.

Receiving to Rest

by Susanna Parent

"For rest they have a perfect restlessness. ... The people are in an emergency to relax." These are lines from Wendell Berry's novel *Jayber Crow*, the author of whom is also an environmental activist and a long-time farmer. I was struck by these words and how Jayber's character spoke of people seeking a false kind of rest. You see, Jayber lives near the river. Sounds peaceful, doesn't it? Yet on the weekends, he sees his river stirred up "like a spoon in a cup of coffee." On the weekends he sees people longing to experience the peacefulness of the great outdoors, but in order to do this, they move along quite hastily. They travel with great speed both in their cars and on their boats, play their music loud enough to mask the sound of their boat's motor, and can never sit in one place too long, for fear that the fish are biting more somewhere else. These people are not slowing down to receive what is around them, but rather grasping to try to maximize their experience of what they believe rest to be. How do you define rest? Does your daily life provide you with moments of rest? As one season begins to morph into another, we are provided with our own fresh opportunity for transformation. A time to reflect upon our rhythm of life and any changes we may want to make.

While the frigid temperatures of wintertime may not provide any available gardens or fields for sauntering, this brisk season does bring other delights to bask in. Take, for example, the dazzling sparkle of the morning sun's reflection in the snow, or the soft snowflakes seen falling beneath the glow of a lamppost in the evening. Each of these moments can be easily overlooked, but if you slow down enough to just take a few seconds to gaze out your window, you might find yourself drawn into the beauty and wonder of it all. As Josef Pieper wrote in his well-known book, *Leisure, the Basis of Culture*, "When we really let our minds rest contemplatively on a rose in bud, on a child at play, on a divine mystery, we are rested and quickened as though by a dreamless sleep."

"Let everything in creation draw you to God. Refresh your mind with some innocent recreation and needful rest, if it were only to saunter through the garden or the fields, listening to the sermon preached by the flowers, the trees, the meadows, the sun, the sky, and the whole universe. You will find that they exhort you to love and praise God; that they excite you to extol the greatness of the Sovereign Architect Who has given them their being."

— St. Paul of the Cross

There are a variety of ways one can find rest. The favorites of St. Thomas Aquinas likely included his own suggestions of "good sleep, a bath, and a glass of wine." True rest can also be found in leisure. As Pieper writes, "leisure is not the attitude of the one who intervenes but of the one who opens himself; not of someone who seizes but of one who lets himself go." Leisure is about being present and receiving the world around you. It is also about opening oneself up to what the Lord has for you.

To enjoy a morning in your home, warming your hands with a mug of hot coffee or tea and watching the colors of nature start to pop as the sun rises higher in the sky. This is leisure. Idleness or sloth, on the other hand, is a lack of calm or interior peace. It looks more like waking up in the morning, mindlessly sipping your hot beverage, while scrolling through your phone. Idleness tends toward an escape, whereas leisure leads you into a deeper experience of reality.

If you are feeling overwhelmed with where to start incorporating more rest into your life, I suggest starting with the Sabbath. "Therefore, a Sabbath rest remains for the people of God. And whoever enters into God's rest, rests from his works as God did from his" (Hebrews 4:9-10). Dr. Michael Naughton, author of *Getting Work Right: Labor & Leisure in a Fragmented World*, says that the Sabbath "is written into creation itself, this idea of rhythm, patterns of creation, and the need to re-calibrate. We anchor our week, we let go, give things back to God, and trust in God's providence that He will take care of things." How can we anchor the week on this day of celebrating the Sabbath?

Making a Wreath with Fresh Greenery

If you love crafty projects, this is an easy DIY to do with a friend or you can even host a little wreath-making gathering with some warm, cozy drinks. Bring the glorious smell of a forest into your home with this fun and simple way to decorate and prepare for the holiday festivities.

What you'll need:

- A wreath hoop: either a minimal gold hoop, brown grapevine wreath, or even a wood embroidery hoop
- Floral wire
- Wire cutter
- Floral clippers
- 2-3 varieties of greenery
- Red holly berries, peppercorns, or tallow berries (optional)
- Dehydrated citrus slices, pinecones, pomegranates, herb clippings (optional)
- Velvet ribbon (optional)

You can find different types of wreath hoops at your local craft store. For the greenery, you can grab a bunch of evergreen clippings in the scrap bin at a local Christmas tree farm, although they do dry out rather quickly. Pre-cut garlands of cedar branches are usually sold at several stores around the holidays and dry out well. If you'd like to use greenery that won't dry out and will last beyond the season, you can find preserved evergreen branches online. Some other types of foliage you can use that dry well: seeded eucalyptus, bay leaves, grevillea, and nandina. If you have a garden to forage, feel free to cut your own foliage! Place fresh greenery in water until you are ready to create your wreath. The possibilities are endless, so get creative!

Instructions:

1. Envision the style of your wreath. Do you prefer a more traditional look or more minimal and simple look with an asymmetrical shape?

2. Create small bunches of a variety of different greenery clippings.

3. Lay one bunch at a time on the hoop and attach tightly to the stems with floral wire. Be sure to slightly layer the bunches a little to hide the wire, facing the same direction.

4. You can cover the entire hoop or leave some of it exposed, per your personal preference. You can keep it super simple or add sprigs of red berries over the greenery.

5. As the final touch, you can embellish with dehydrated citrus slices, mini pinecones, or small pomegranates. Either attach with hot glue or wire. If you'd like, tie velvet ribbons from the top and let them hang.

6. Using twine or ribbon, hang on your front door, window, or a wall inside. You can also give it as a gift to a friend or neighbor.

Tip: Spritz the back of your wreath with water every few days to keep it fresh longer and bring out the fragrance.

Waiting in Winter

by Mackenzie Worthing

Winter is a time of stillness. The earth is quiet, often covered in snow. The grass does not grow. Flowers do not show colorful, friendly faces rising up out of the earth. The days can feel long, though the hours of sunshine are short and more often than not clouded over with thick gray clouds. Gloom can settle into the heart if we allow it. But there is a tenderness in this stillness because there's the opportunity to wait. In a world that values efficiency, haste, and getting things done faster than ever, we seldom have opportunities to truly wait and lean into the waiting. The cold, dreary months of winter provide us with several months of waiting for warmer, sunnier days ahead.

Although waiting for something is not itself a virtue, there are virtues consonant with the practice of waiting: patience and hope. Patience is the virtue of suffering well. We usually have a watered-down understanding of this virtue, but the Latin word that we take our English one from, *patientia*, is the quality of suffering with endurance. Hope is also a virtue that we water down as some kind of fuzzy, feel-good cheerful feeling for the future, but it is in fact a theological virtue. Theological virtues have as both their origin and their end God Himself. Hope, then, is the desire for and expectation of salvation by the gift of God's grace. Winter gives us the opportunity to grow in patience by suffering the cold and the inconveniences it provides (physical discomfort, having to dress small children in a thousand layers to go outside, shoveling snow, the inability to grow produce, etc.). Winter also gives us the opportunity to grow in hope in the theological sense as we await the celebration of Easter and hope in the wider sense of looking forward to the glories of spring. We can look to the saints for examples of the virtues of patience and hope to help us carry our burdens throughout the season of winter or in other seasons of life that entail great waiting.

"Be patient, therefore, brethren, until the coming of the Lord. Behold, the
farmer waits for the precious fruit of the earth, being patient over it until it
receives the early and the late rain. You also be patient. Establish your hearts,
for the coming of the Lord is at hand."

— James 5:7-8

A particular feast in the midst of winter gives us shining examples of saints who waited with patience and hope for the fulfillment of the Lord's promises: Candlemas. Celebrated on February 2nd, Candlemas, also known as the Feast of the Presentation, is a literal light in the darkness. In the traditional calendar, it marked the end of the Christmas season and gave the faithful a chance to have candles blessed by the priest at Mass, hence the name "Candle-mass." The feast comes from the story of Jesus' Presentation in the Temple in the Gospel of St. Luke. Mary and Joseph bring the Child Jesus to the Temple to redeem Him according to the law of Moses. In the Temple the Holy Family encounter Simeon, who is described as "righteous and devout, looking for the consolation of Israel, and the Holy Spirit was upon him" (Luke 2:25). Essentially, Simeon is painted as one who was waiting for the Messiah and is described the way the great saints of the Old Testament are described: as having the Holy Spirit upon him. In fact, he had such an intimate relationship with the Holy Spirit that it had been revealed that he "should not see death before he had seen the Lord's Christ" (26).

We do not know how long Simeon waited. What we do know is that he waited faithfully and trusted in what had been revealed to him. And when the time was fulfilled according to divine providence, Simeon showed up in the Temple led by the Holy Spirit and without reservation took the infant Jesus in his arms. And as he looked upon the sweet face of this baby, he knew he beheld the "consolation of Israel" — the Divine Consoler. With that blessed child clasped to his chest, he proclaimed a beautiful canticle testifying to God's fulfillment of His promises,

> "Lord, now let your servant depart in peace according to your word;
> for my eyes have seen your salvation,
> which you have prepared in the presence of all peoples,
> a light for revelation to the Gentiles,
> and for glory to your people Israel." (29-32)

This prophetic song indicates that Simeon is now prepared for death, having seen the one through whom salvation is to come. The mere presence of Jesus, a sleepy, dependent babe, was enough to satiate the years of waiting this man had done. It was enough for him to glimpse the hope of the world. Simeon's canticle, known by its Latin title *Nunc dimittis*, has been prayed daily for the office of Compline in the Liturgy of the Hours for centuries. It serves as a reminder to those who pray it that the Lord has provided them with another day to remember and revel in Christ's salvific love. Simeon's prophecy does not conclude with his canticle. He turns to the Blessed Mother and to her reveals still more — that this little "light to the Gentiles" and "glory of Israel" will also bring with Him division that will leave her own heart pierced with a sword that "the thoughts of many might be revealed" (34-35). Mary is also a saint worthy of our contemplation here as waiting with patience and hope. Her heart will be pierced — she will suffer on behalf of her Son — but all for the glory of God and for the revelation of truth. In this must be her hope for the future of the little child nuzzled against her. He has come to save His people — and save them He will.

Finally, following Simeon's prophetic utterances, a holy widow, Anna, approaches. In her ripe old age, she has spent most of her life as a widow and she "did not depart from the temple, worshipping with fasting and prayer night and day" (37). Though she might not have had quite the intimacy with the Holy Spirit with which Simeon is described, this prayer warrior of a woman is described as a prophetess, who on beholding the scene of the Holy Family with Simeon, "gave thanks to God, and spoke of him to all who were looking for the redemption of Israel" (38). In other words, she too recognized the Christ Child as the Messiah, the one who would redeem Israel. She endured her widowhood with patient and dedicated prayer before the Lord in the Temple. And as soon as she beheld Jesus, she proclaimed with hope her expectation of the deliverance of the people. Simeon, Mary, and Anna are saints to whom we can look for strength in persevering in patience and hope through whatever season of waiting we are in. Whether it is simply the gloomy days of winter waiting on spring, waiting for a baby to be born, waiting to get pregnant, waiting to discern a vocation, waiting to heal, waiting for the world to look a little less grim, or waiting on the Lord to fulfill a promise He has laid on our hearts, we can ask these saints of holy waiting to pray for us. May they intercede on our behalf that we, like them, may wait with steadfastness of heart, trusting that the Lord will fulfill His promises.

Cozy Winter Drinks

by Marisa Fredrickson

Throughout the winter season, coffee shops are rolling out drinks full of syrups that are made with less-than-wholesome ingredients. Here are three festive alternatives that can be made simply at home, using real ingredients. Any of these can be stirred into coffee, tea, or hot milk — whatever your preference is!

Gingerbread Syrup:

- 1 cup maple syrup
- 1/2 cup water
- 3/4 tsp ground ginger
- 1/2 tsp cinnamon
- 1/4 tsp fresh ground nutmeg
- 1/4 tsp ground cloves
- 1 tsp vanilla extract

Winter Spice Syrup:

- 1 orange, juiced and zested
- 1 cup maple syrup
- 1/2 cup water
- 1/2 tsp cinnamon
- 1/4 tsp cardamom
- 1 tsp vanilla extract

Instructions for the Syrups:

1. Begin by whisking together the ingredients (wait to add the vanilla) of your chosen syrup in a saucepan over medium heat.

2. Allow the syrup to come to a boil, then lower the heat to a simmer.

3. Continue stirring often until the syrup has reduced by a third and thickened. Strain any spices or zest, stir in the vanilla, and store in a glass jar when cool. These syrups will keep for 1 month in the fridge.

Winter Spice Syrup:

- 1 cup maple syrup
- 1/2 cup whole milk
- 1/3 cup cocoa powder
- 1/4 cup dark chocolate or cacao, chopped
- 1 tsp vanilla
- 1 tsp peppermint extract

Instructions for the Syrup:

1. Whisk together the maple syrup and milk in a saucepan over medium heat, bringing it to a simmer. Once simmering, whisk in the cocoa powder and dark chocolate, then reduce the heat slightly. Continue cooking and stirring until the syrup has reduced slightly.

2. Stir in the extracts and store in a glass jar when cool. Because we are using real chocolate, some separation may occur as it sits in the fridge. All it needs is a quick stir before using! This sauce will keep for 2 weeks in the fridge.

Cultivating a Holy Silence in Our Home

by Theresa Thomas

Frost upon a windowpane and softly falling snow, books and blankets, steaming hot drinks, the sacred silence of a frozen earth, the soft glow of an ember on a candlelit cozy night. These all make up the magical and holy feeling of a home in winter. There are two different types of winter seasons. The first is the secular winter holiday season full of impulsive shopping, holiday travel, endless parties, the receiving of gift after gift, and a complete whirlwind of activities. The other season is a sacred and spiritual time, a slow and beautiful anticipatory lead-up to our Savior's birth followed by many days and weeks of celebration. As a Catholic homemaker, I take on the responsibility of creating and setting the tone in our home. Especially in the Christmas season, I try to cultivate a holy silence in my own heart and our home in order to guide our minds to the sacred and prepare our hearts for Our Lord's birth.

Reign in the Insatiable Appetite for News

We haven't watched the news in our home for years. But this point also includes web surfing on our phones and trying to keep up with all the bustle of friends and acquaintances on every social media platform. We gorge ourselves with the curiosity and the news of others, which distracts us from being present with our families. This also applies to feeling the need to update everyone virtually on our own lives. "All the rivers run into the sea, yet the sea is not full…. the eye is not satisfied with seeing, nor the ear filled with hearing" (Ecclesiastes 1: 7-8b). Although the world is a place that screams for more and feels entitled to always having information within seconds, by creating an absence of this noise we allow the Lord to sustain our deep longing for information. We get the opportunity to intimately engage with Our Lord about our daily struggles and joys, because He is truly all we need.

> "Wisdom enters through love, silence, and mortification. It is great wisdom to know how to be silent and to look at neither the remarks, nor the deeds, nor the lives of others."
>
> — St. John of the Cross

Quiet Conversations with Our Lord

Adoration is one of the most beautiful forms of prayer. Not to depreciate the beauty and graces that come from adoring Our Lord in Eucharistic Adoration, but Jesus is still with us and we are still able to adore and converse intimately with Him throughout our normal daily life! My favorite time to pray is in the silence of the morning before anyone in the house has awoken, but with different seasons of life, it isn't always feasible for me to get out of bed to do this. Instead, I asked myself the questions: "Are there moments in my day that I am filling with unimportant noise? Am I always listening to the latest podcast, another audiobook, music, or other background noise?" The answers were yes.

For me as a busy mother, I often felt like I was not doing enough if I wasn't multitasking, if I was just tending to the children, just cooking, just cleaning, just driving to the next errand. However, those daily duties are holy work. They are enough and can be offered up! There are so many lovely quiet moments in motherhood that can be made even more beautiful if you use them as a time of worship. A silent conversation with Our Lord while you wash the dishes, a prayer of thanksgiving for your family while you nurse the baby back to sleep, a contemplative prayer while you sweep the kitchen floor for the third time that day or fold a load of laundry. All of these small pockets of time can be tender meditative moments or devotional time spent with God.

Silent Night, Holy Night

As Catholic women and homemakers, we have no one better to imitate than our Blessed Mother with her examples of holy silence and intimate conversations with her Son. I often ponder how she would have kept her home, mothered and spoken to Jesus each day, and been a helpmate to St. Joseph. When my husband comes home during Advent and especially the Christmas season, I want him to come home to a home of peace and solitude. A home that gives him a break from the chaos of the world and the secular bustle. Evenings in a peaceful home often remind me of the beautiful way that the Christmas night was depicted by Joseph Mohr, "Silent night, holy night, all is calm, all is bright." Our hidden years filled with sacred moments spent mothering and homemaking are not in vain or wasted away. Your time with these sweet souls entrusted to your care is important, valuable, and holy work. May your little daily duties of love be a prayer rising to Him, and may you find time in this winter season to cultivate a holy silence and make room in your heart for intimate conversations with Our Savior.

"Contemplative prayer in my opinion is nothing else than a close
sharing between friends; it means taking time frequently to be
alone with Him who we know loves us."

— St. Teresa of Ávila

Speculaas Cookies

for the feast of St. Nicholas (December 6)

by Marisa Fredrickson

Spice Mix Ingredients:

- 8 Tbsp cinnamon
- 2 Tbsp nutmeg
- 1 1/2 Tbsp cloves
- 1 Tbsp dried ginger
- 2 tsp cardamom
- 2 tsp aniseed
- 1 tsp mace (optional)
- 1 tsp black pepper

Cookie Ingredients:

- 16 Tbsp salted butter, room temperature
- 3/4 cup cane sugar
- 1/4 cup brown sugar
- 1 1/2 Tbsp speculaas spice mix
- 1 tsp almond extract
- 3 Tbsp milk
- 3 cups + 2 Tbsp all-purpose flour (substitute gluten-free if needed)
- 1/4 tsp baking powder

These delightful spiced cookies have been made in Belgium and the Netherlands since the 17th century. While their exact origin can be argued, it is said that in lieu of handing out images of St. Nicholas for his feast day, monks began to carve his image into wooden molds that were pressed with dough and baked.

Instructions:

1. In a mixing bowl, beat together the butter and sugar until pale and fluffy. Stir in the milk and almond extract.

2. Whisk together the flour, spice mix, and baking powder, then add to the creamed butter and stir until combined.

3. Shape the dough into a ball, place it in an airtight container, and let it rest in the fridge for 1 hour.

4. Preheat the oven to 350 degrees and prepare a baking sheet with parchment paper or a silicone mat.

5. Cutting and shaping the cookies will vary based on the tools that you have. If you have wooden molds, they can be lightly dusted with flour and dough can be pressed into them. The dough can also be rolled out and cut into circles or squares that are stamped with a press, or left as simple and delicious shapes.

6. Placing the tray of cookies in the freezer for 10 minutes prior to baking will help maintain the details in stamped or pressed cookies.

7. Bake for about 10 minutes, or until the surface looks completely dry. Allow the cookies to cool completely on a wire rack before storing at room temperature. These will stay fresh for several days.

The Many Gifts of Bees

Absolutely critical to our ecosystem, bees also have a unique place in Catholic culture. Honeybees were traditionally a sign of hard work, order, vigilance, and diligence. It seems that the bee was also associated with chastity, or virginity. There are several saints whose patronage includes bees, beekeeping, and/or candle making: St. Ambrose, St. Benedict, St. Bernard of Clairvaux, St. Dominic, and even St. Valentine. Each of their stories are worth diving into! Bee products have been used and loved for thousands of years, and Scripture alludes to their sweetness with frequent references to the "land flowing with milk and honey." When it comes to our health, there are more gifts from this tiny flying insect than we may realize.

Note: Sourcing of bee products is very important — not just for quality, but for the impact it has on bee communities. When harvesting these superfoods, it is imperative that the bee hive be cared for and left with enough resources to continue thriving.

Raw Honey

Raw honey is the unfiltered and unpasteurized substance that bees make from the nectar of flowers. This natural sweetener is universally loved and heralded as the simplest go-to for a tickle in the throat. But its benefits and uses go far beyond the common cold. It has many uses topically in wound healing or addressing other skin concerns. Internally, it performs many actions in supporting immune health, digestive/gut health, blood sugar, sleep, and energy.

Bee Pollen

Bee pollen, while not as famous as honey, is a mixture of flower pollen, nectar, bees' digestive enzymes, and wax. It is formed when bees fly from flower to flower, pack it into pellets, and carry it back to the hive. Although bee pollen is small, it is a powerhouse of vitamins, minerals, amino acids, and antioxidants. Bee pollen supports our metabolism, reduces inflammation, boosts immunity, supports the histamine response, and more.

> "Meditation is made, we may say, as the bees make honey; for they make it by gathering the dew that falls from heaven upon the flowers, and drawing a little juice from these flowers, which they change into honey, and then carry to their hives. Thus we go over and over the life of our Lord in meditation, taking up one action after another, and considering them, in order to compose the honey of holy virtues, and draw from them the graces of a holy meditation."
>
> —St. Francis de Sales

Bee Propolis

Some consider this their secret weapon for winter wellness. Propolis is made when bees combine tree resin (and other sources) with their salivary secretions (plus beeswax). It is a source of prebiotics and antioxidants, while also being antifungal and antibacterial. It improves intestinal barrier functions and protects against oxidative stress. While it is a valuable part of your standard illness protocol, it is also used as a helpful support when battling mold toxicity or other complex illnesses.

Royal Jelly

Royal jelly is a bee secretion from nurse bees that contains amino acids required for cell growth and reproduction. It is "royal" because it is food for the queen bee herself! The queen bee (along with larvae, baby bees) is fed royal jelly nearly *exclusively*, contributing to her tremendously long life and larger size. It is antibacterial, immune supporting, and rich in antioxidants.

Beeswax

Beeswax improves air quality and releases negative ions, helping to clear the air of allergens, mold spores, bacteria, and viruses. Traditionally, it was required that altar candles were to be made primarily of pure beeswax. While this has somewhat changed over time, the use of beeswax for the Liturgy is still prevalent and carries great meaning as expressed above. There is likely still much to be discovered about bees as well as their gifts to nature and humans alike. That said, we know enough to know their value and potential benefit to understand the importance of protecting bees and thanking God for their many uses.

Honey Crème Brûlée

for the feast of St. Ambrose (December 7)

by Marisa Fredrickson

Yields 4 servings.

Ingredients:

- 2 cups heavy whipping cream
- 4 Tbsp honey
- 4 Tbsp cane or maple sugar
- 1 vanilla bean, split lengthwise, or 1 tsp vanilla extract
- 1/8 tsp salt
- 5 egg yolks
- Cane sugar for topping

The story goes that when St. Ambrose was just an infant, a swarm of bees landed on his face and left behind a drop of honey. To his father, this was a sign that Ambrose would become someone great with a wonderful sense for speaking.

Instructions:

1. Preheat oven to 325 degrees.

2. Combine honey, vanilla bean, salt, and cream in a saucepan over low heat, just until the mixture becomes hot. If using vanilla bean, it can now be discarded. If using vanilla extract, add it in now.

3. While the milk is warming, beat together the egg yolks and sugar until light and frothy. Slowly pour the milk into the egg yolk mixture, 1/4 cup at a time. This process is called "tempering" and helps prevent the eggs from scrambling. Pour the custard into four 6-ounce ramekins, or one 8x8 baking dish. Place the ramekins into another baking dish, and fill the dish with boiling water until it reaches halfway up the sides of the ramekins. Bake for 30-40 minutes or until the tops are barely set. Allow to cool slightly before refrigerating for at least a few hours, or up to 2 days.

4. When you are ready to serve, sprinkle the tops with enough cane sugar to cover the surface, then broil in the oven (or torch, if you have one!) until the sugar has melted and browned. The crème brûlée can be topped with a bit of honeycomb or bee pollen, or served as is.

Instant Pot Barbacoa

for the feast of Our Lady of Guadalupe (December 12)

by Marisa Fredrickson

Yields 8 servings.

Ingredients:

- Oil for cooking
- 3-4-lb chuck roast, cut into 4 pieces
- 1 1/2 Tbsp cumin
- 1/2 Tbsp onion powder
- 1/2 Tbsp garlic powder
- 1 Tbsp oregano
- 1 Tbsp paprika
- 1 Tbsp chili powder
- Salt and pepper, to taste
- 2 bay leaves
- 14.5-oz can fire roasted tomatoes
- 1 1/2 cups beef or broth
- Cilantro, white onion, limes, and radish for serving

Instructions:

1. Turn Instant Pot to sauté mode and add enough oil to coat the bottom of the pot.

2. Season the roast with all of the spices, then brown the chunks on each side. Add in the fire roasted tomatoes, broth, and bay leaves.

3. Cover and set your Instant Pot to high pressure for 90 minutes. When the roast is done cooking, quick release (natural release is fine too!).

4. Remove the meat to shred, and top with a few pours of the cooking broth. Season with more salt, as desired. Any leftover broth can be used for cooking rice and does not need to be strained, but bay leaves should be discarded.

Sankta Lucia

by Maria Fredriksson

F ar, far away in the Northlands of Scandinavia when the December days have become short and frosty and the winter nights very long and frozen, there comes a night — *Luciadagen* — when Catholics and Protestants alike remember the martyr Sankta Lucia on her feast day, December 13th.

Her celebration is so vital in Scandinavia — particularly Sweden — partly because she has one of the oldest cults of devotion in Christian Europe and partly because her name means "Light" and has extra symbolism in both the darkness of winter and in the days leading up to the Nativity of the Light of the World. As with many old cultures, the festivities of her day are mixed with leftover wisps of paganism from when Nordic cultures believed that December 13th was the night when Lusse (a wicked witch) and many ghosts wandered the world freely and many people stayed up all night to keep their fires lit and hence keep them away. St. Lucy being a bearer of Light would have become the Christian gift that chased away those spirits by bringing warmth, cheer, food, light, and the Faith.

In Scandinavia now, the custom is for the eldest daughter of the house to rise early and awaken the rest of the family with a tray of *Lussekatter* (saffron buns) and black coffee as she walks through the house dressed in white with a red sash, wearing a green head wreath with seven white candles, and singing the "Sankta Lucia" song. Later in the day there is often a Lucia Crown Cake — a coffee cake shaped like a crown with seven candles in it — and *glögg* (mulled wine). This is a custom still carried on in many parts of the United States settled by Scandinavian immigrants, particularly in the Midwest. As this custom became more widely popular within Protestant Scandinavia in Europe, it evolved into processions through town or in concerts where Sankta Lucia is accompanied by whole choirs of girls in white and Star Boys dressed in white with conical hats with stars, the passing out of white candles on this darkest day of the year, and the customary refreshments of *Lussekatter* and *glögg*.

"The words of the living God cannot be suppressed or put to silence."

— St. Lucy

Lussekatter (Saffron Buns)

for the feast of St. Lucy (December 13)
by Maria Fredriksson

Yields 12 servings.

Ingredients:

- 3/4 cup milk
- 1/2 tsp saffron threads*
- 1 tsp plus 1/4 cup of white granulated sugar
- 1 1/4-ounce packet of active dry yeast
- 3 1/2-4 cups all-purpose flour
- 1/2 tsp salt
- 1/4 cup unsalted butter, room temperature
- 1/4 cup sour cream (or quark if available)
- 2 large eggs
- 2 raisins per bun (about 24)
- 1 egg, beaten for glaze

**The reason saffron was a special ingredient was because it was a flavorful, costly spice and so only used at this time of year.*

Instructions:

1. Soak raisins in bowl of water. Heat milk, saffron, and 1 teaspoon of sugar until milk is steamy and sugar dissolved. Cool until warm to touch but not hot.

2. Sprinkle yeast over the milk and let sit 5-10 minutes until foamy. Whisk 3 1/2 cups flour, remaining sugar, and salt together. Make a well in the center of dry mix and add the milk mixture, eggs, butter, and sour cream. Mix until well incorporated.

3. Knead the dough, adding additional flour a tablespoon at a time until dough is a little sticky but does not stick to hands. Shape into a ball, place in a large bowl, cover, and let rise in a warm place until dough has doubled in size. Gently press down and knead a couple of times.

4. Break off pieces into balls about 2 inches wide. Roll each ball into a snake about 14 inches long and then curl the ends in opposite directions to form an "S" with curls at each end. Place on lined baking sheets and let dough sit covered for 30 minutes for second rise.

5. Preheat oven to 400 degrees, brush each shape with the beaten egg, and push a raisin into the center of each spiral (2 per "S"). Bake for 10-11 minutes, turning trays halfway through, until buns are golden brown. Cool for 5 minutes before eating.

Christmas Cookies

by Marisa Fredrickson

Yields about 40 cookies.

Cookie ingredients:

- 8 oz cream cheese, room temperature
- 2 cups salted butter, room temperature
- 2 cups cane sugar
- 2 egg yolks
- 2 tsp vanilla
- 5 1/4 cups flour*

**For gluten-free cookies, substitute 5 cups gluten-free flour and 1/4 cup arrowroot or tapioca starch.*

Frosting ingredients:

- 1 cup salted butter
- 3 cups powdered sugar
- 1 tsp vanilla
- 1 Tbsp cream

Instructions:

Using a stand or hand mixer, combine all ingredients, mixing gently at first, and then increase speed once everything is combined. Mix for 5 minutes on medium, and then finish on low to smooth out air bubbles.

Cookie instructions:

1. Using a stand or hand mixer, cream together butter and cream cheese until smooth. Sprinkle in sugar and mix on medium speed for a few minutes, then add in egg yolks and vanilla. Add flour in batches to lessen the mess, and mix on low just until everything is combined.

2. Chill your dough for at least 2 hours before rolling out cookies.

3. Preheat oven to 350 degrees. Roll out your dough on a lightly floured surface, or between 2 sheets of parchment paper, until it's about 1/2" thick. Cut out desired shapes, and bake for 10-12 minutes. The tops will look dry, and the edges should be barely golden.

Tip: if making gluten-free cookies, chill your cut-out shapes in the fridge for about 15 minutes prior to baking. This isn't necessary, but helps keep the edges crisp.

Christmas Cookies — Natural Food Coloring

There are many reasons to avoid artificial food coloring, and thankfully we're able to achieve beautiful hues using food- and plant-based coloring! Color Garden and TruColor are two brands of plant-based colors that do not yield an off taste and have many vibrant color options. Here is a list of some natural powders that can be used to make a rainbow of colors. Mixing these with just a touch of hot water will help the powder to dissolve into a paste and incorporate smoothly into your frosting.

Red/Pink:	Orange:	Yellow:	Green:	Blue:	Purple:
beet, pitaya, hibiscus	*carrot, paprika*	*turmeric*	*green spirulina, matcha*	*blue spirulina, butterfly pea powder (blue matcha)*	*butterfly pea powder + lemon juice*

Black/grey: food-grade charcoal, black cocoa (classic Oreo taste)

Brown: cocoa powder

Tip: the color of your frosting will deepen over time, so don't worry if it feels a bit pale at first. You may just need more time, and not color. A sprinkle of cocoa powder adds a lovely softness to colors as well and works perfectly for creating natural evergreen hues.

Joy Beyond Christmas Day

by Mackenzie Worthing

At the beginning of what may be a bleak winter comes a joyous holiday: Christmas. The word alone inspires hope and whimsy. Even those who are not Christian usually have a softness for the Christmas season, with its general jolliness, beautiful displays, and air of gratitude and generosity. The trouble is that the secular celebration seems to end somewhere in the evening hours of December 25th. The world spends an awful lot of time preparing for Christmas, but in the wrong timeframe and with the wrong outlook. They are preparing for gift-giving and food-sharing and perhaps inevitable family bickering, but they are not preparing for, nor truly reveling in, the "reason for the season" — the birth of Jesus Christ. The Incarnation and Birth of God-made-man is the incomparable reason why we celebrate. Without the Word becoming Flesh, the death and Resurrection could not have taken place. Though God's salvific plan was in motion from the very moment of the Fall, the entrance of the Second Person of the Trinity into the world to save us sinners was the definitive turning point in Salvation History. God, infinite in power and majesty, became a wee babe who nursed at His mother's breast. What wonder! How can it be that Our Lord would come to us in such a way? He determined it was the best way to save us, to become one of us. There was an infinite divide created by Adam and Eve's disobedience and only one who was infinite could cross it. Yet only man could adequately pay reparation for the sins of man. Thus Jesus, Son of God and Son of Mary, was born in a stable in Bethlehem to fulfill the prophecies foretold to God's chosen people. We have immense reason to celebrate this. We not only have a reason, but we have an obligation to celebrate Christmas not only with all due solemnity but with zeal and joy!

Secular Christmas begins too early and ends too soon. In the Church, we have the four-week season of Advent to help us prepare for Christmas. Then Christmastide begins with Christmas Day and traditionally goes until February 2nd, the Feast of the Presentation. In the new calendar, Christmas officially begins on Christmas Day and concludes 12 days later with the feast of Epiphany. This is something else the world gets backwards — the 12 days of Christmas. Most use this misunderstood phrase to mean a countdown to Christmas, rather than the true celebration that starts with and follows from Christmas Day. The first eight days of the twelve days of Christmas are the Christmas Octave. In the Church, we have always celebrated major solemnities with octaves, meaning that the week following the feast is as though another day of the feast itself. Traditionally, the season of Christmas would last until what is now known as the Feast of the Presentation, but is also known as Candlemas and the Purification of the Blessed Virgin Mary, on February 2nd.

The season of joyful hope is meant to carry us through the darker days of winter, to help us turn our hearts towards the Light of the World, Jesus Christ Himself. The call to truly celebrate Christmastide comes with a few practical caveats as well. It is primarily in our prayers above all that we ought to be joyfully offering praise to our God. It is not prudent or sustainable for us to gift-give and eat the way we usually do on December 25th itself. There are, however, many other ways in which we can incorporate the spirit of truly holistic celebrations — that of the body and of the soul — throughout the twelve days and beyond toward February 2nd. Some general ideas for body and soul are given below with a chart of feasts and specific feast-day ideas following. No matter how or what way you celebrate the Christmas season, may it all be inspired by an abiding faith in the love that the Lord has for you. For you alone He would have become man and suffered His cruel death. He died for the sins of all men, but He would have done it for you and you alone. May this thought, this wondrous, beautiful thought, encourage you to celebrate Christmastide with ever-new awe and joy!

Body and Soul

- Plan one or two special and nourishing foods to enjoy each day.
- Go on Rosary walks with family and friends, meditating on the Joyful Mysteries.
- Listen to or watch a performance of Handel's *Messiah*.
- Space out gift-giving so there isn't overwhelm on Christmas Day, especially if you have little children: some families do stockings on Christmas Eve, a big/family gift on Christmas Day, and then open other gifts on Epiphany to commemorate the gifts brought by the Wise Men.
- Read a book of reflections on the mystery of the Incarnation by a saint.
- Continue to light your Advent wreath with the addition of a white candle in the center.
- Consider waiting to decorate your Christmas tree until Christmas Eve — also known as the feast of Adam and Eve.
- Light candles or extra candles for your daily prayers.
- Make something to share with your neighbors — cookies, bread, a tea or hot chocolate blend — and include a holy card of the Christ Child or the Holy Family with the gift.
- Either make a space for a home altar or set aside special Christmastide decorations for your existing home altar.
- Go look at Christmas lights around town with Christmas hymns playing.
- Go to Mass/adoration as often as possible to give glory to God for his "marvelous exchange."
- Host a "Twelve Days" Dinner with a twelve-course menu (could be partially brought by guests!) and perhaps some music and dancing.
- Wait to take down Christmas decorations until after Epiphany (January 6) or the Presentation (February 2).

Rosary Reflections for Winter

by Emily Patteson

As the days get colder and darker during this winter season, it is easy to feel like it is simply a season to endure. In this set of Rosary reflections on the joyful mysteries, we ask for Our Lady's intercession as we seek to embrace the season and grow closer to Jesus Christ. Outside, the world can look dormant and bleak. As we retreat into our homes, may we also retreat into our hearts with expectation for what the Lord will do. Let us seek to be united to Mary as she waits in anticipation for the coming of her Son, Our Lord Jesus.

Opening prayer: Lord, as I seek the shelter of my home in this season of winter, I ask that You would fill my heart with that same warmth. I seek to be open to how You are moving in this season, even when it is in the most unexpected ways. Open my heart to be moved in this time of prayer that I may experience Your joy and hope in this season of winter. Amen.

The Annunciation

"Mary said, 'Behold, I am the handmaid of the Lord. May it be done to me according to your word.'" (Luke 1:38)

Lord, You teach us, by the example of Mary, to lovingly accept Your will and trust that You are moving in the silence of our hearts and lives. Even in the invisible work of pregnancy, she knew that You were working something great inside her. *Help us to trust that You work in the silence of our hearts.*

Some seasons of life can feel like winter — long, barren roads that must be trod. We cannot question the road even though we might not see progress. This stage that Mary is in is one of simply coming to accept the plan and promise that has been spoken. She rests, knowing that though progress cannot be outwardly seen, the path is worth taking. *What are you enduring in your life right now that may feel barren or lacking progress? Ask the Lord to help you trust in His silent progress and keep on the road.*

The Visitation

"During those days Mary set out and traveled to the hill country in haste to a town of Judah, where she entered the house of Zechariah and greeted Elizabeth." (Luke 1:39-40)

Mary made haste to see her cousin Elizabeth and teaches us that we must orient our hearts toward loving others. The orientation of our hearts can affect how we see things, how we act, and how we interact with others. *Lord, teach me how to orient my life to be a gift of love for my friends and family.*

An important lesson we must learn is to love others as we love ourselves. Firstly, we want to ensure that we do indeed love ourselves. This means being gentle and caring, rather than harsh when we make mistakes. It also means taking care of our needs and seeing them as valid and worthy of caring for. When we have the right attitude toward ourselves, we can have the same attitude toward others, with a greater capacity to love them. *Are you better at loving yourself or loving others? How can you work toward a balance to follow the command of loving others as self?*

The Birth of Jesus

"'Behold, the virgin shall be with child and bear a son, and they shall name him Emmanuel,' which means 'God is with us.'" (Matthew 1:23)

Jesus, Your birth was long awaited and brought light to a broken and hurting world full of darkness and sin. In one single moment, everything changed. It was such a silent moment that few people even knew something was different. *Help us to recognize that Your presence in our lives changes everything and let us anticipate the life You bring.*

All around us in nature we see the dormant ground, lifeless. Maybe this season of your life feels this way as well. What if we look with eyes of anticipation instead? For example, we may look at a pregnant mother and see the life that will soon be on earth and in the arms of the family. Let us see the growth and beauty that this dormant time is preparing the ground for. *How might looking at your life with the eyes of anticipation change your perspective on what you are going through right now?*

The Presentation of Jesus in the Temple

"[T]hey took him up to Jerusalem to present him to the Lord, just as it is written in the law of the Lord, 'Every male that opens the womb shall be consecrated to the Lord.'" (Luke 2:22-23)

Jesus, You were offered to Your Father in the Temple because of the obedience of Mary and Joseph. They recognized that every good gift comes from above and knew that You belonged to God, not to them. This beautiful act of surrender set the tone for the life of the Holy Family. *Help us to see the gracious gifts You give, God, as Yours, and not our own.*

Just as we wish to hold onto the last green and warm weather of fall or the stage of life we find ourselves in, we tend to clutch our blessings. We do not want to bear the thought of losing them. However, whether we let go or not, we are not in control of our lives, but forcing and pining leads to much angst. Releasing our grasp allows room for God to work out His perfect plan and can bring much peace and freedom. *What is an area of your life where you are trying to control and not letting the Lord work? Choose to trust that God will bring good out of your obedience, just as the beauty of spring always follows winter.*

Finding Jesus in the Temple

"When his parents saw him, they were astonished, and his mother said to him, 'Son, why have you done this to us? Your father and I have been looking for you with great anxiety.' And he said to them, 'Why were you looking for me? Did you not know that I must be in my Father's house?'" (Luke 2:48-49)

Jesus responded to His parents identifying God as His Father, which caused them joy and sorrow: joy in knowing His elevated role and sorrow in the division between them. God is so powerful that He can hold together these opposing feelings, allowing us to experience them both at the same time. We can experience this mingling in times of physical growth or healing. This is paradoxical but also part of the human experience. *Do you focus more on joy or sorrow in your life? What might the Lord be teaching you when He allows you to experience both feelings together?*

Closing prayer: Lord, I thank You for all the ways that You move in my life. Help me to love myself as You love me and orient my life so that love will flow outward to the people around me. I seek to be obedient to You in all things and experience the freedom that comes from giving up control. May You fill my hard days and hard seasons with joy, hope, and expectation. Be with me and warm my life during this winter. Amen.

Embracing Light

There is no denying that sunlight is healing. All life requires the rays of the sun in some way. And yet we are living in a time when people have an unfounded fear of the sun; not because it is being worshipped as it had been in ancient cultures, but due to misinformation combined with poor lifestyles. In summertime, people lather themselves in sunscreen to literally "block" the sun's rays. Yet, in winter, "seasonal affective disorder" runs rampant due to a lack of sun, and those who can will plan a January tropical getaway. It's all very confusing if you try to look at it from a fresh perspective. We know the importance of sunlight for mood, hormone regulation, immunity, vitamin D synthesis, detoxification, sleep, gut health — the list goes on. While some people may live in an area where the sun shines year round, many of us do not have access to optimal sunlight twelve months of the year. For some, there is not enough UV light to synthesize vitamin D for several months out of the year. Then there are those who are living in situations where they are not able to get outside, even when the sun is accessible, whether due to work or another circumstance. While full-spectrum sunlight is always preferable, there are ways to support the body in its natural rhythms, either through embracing a truly seasonal and rhythmic way of life or by adding in supportive therapies. It cannot be overstated, though, that if foundations of health are not being implemented, if circadian rhythm is not supported, if we are not actually getting outside, much of these "supplements" we discuss are pointless. They then become expensive therapies being used as a bandaid for a lifestyle issue that requires lifestyle changes.

A Rhythm for Winter

It takes a bold person to embrace the true nature of winter in today's culture. Because of our fancy devices, our intense pace, our to-do lists, most people are reticent to slowing down in a manner truly compatible with the season. For all my life, I've lived in locations where peak winter sees more darkness than light in a day. The days are so short that it feels unnatural to eat dinner after 5 p.m. Of course, I almost always choose to live in today's pace where I spend a good deal of the dark hours working, doing chores, or in some way trying to extend the day that is no longer there. And we wonder why we get sick more, are often tired, or get the winter blues?

We are not meant to go full throttle this time of year — that's what summer is for. Assuming we got plenty of sunlight throughout the warmer months, we ought to head into winter with high vitamin D stores. Our bodies rely on these stores throughout the cold season, and eventually fall to lows in February or March, ready to be filled up again. When we place high demands on our bodies, in a time when rest should be prioritized, we burn through these stores, ultimately impacting our immune system. Certainly, there's more to the story than vitamin D, but we shouldn't underestimate its importance. If we look at ethnic groups historically living in dark winters, we would see people who consumed fatty fish (rich in vitamin D) for multiple meals a day (not just a few times per week). I wouldn't necessarily advocate that kind of diet today due to toxicities, but it helps us to understand these hearty people who survived long periods of cold. Furthermore, while appropriate UV rays may not be accessible at all times, that doesn't mean we still shouldn't seek out sunlight in winter. Getting outside for at least a few minutes after each meal will still help our moods, blood sugar, and much more.

A Modern Approach to Winter

Sauna Therapy. There was a time when most homes in the far north had a sauna. There is a rich history of sauna use in the Scandinavian countries, and it is simply part of the culture. If you live in a cold climate, finding a way to implement sauna use can be very therapeutic (and maybe even necessary). Warmth is so healing on its own, and adding it where you can in a cold climate is imperative. The additional layer of near-infrared light with sauna makes this an even more powerful therapy. Near-infrared light penetrates the skin and deeper tissues, supporting our mitochondria. It forces our cells to create structured water and is a fantastic support for systemic health.

Fatty Fish Intake. Thriving native cultures in cold places all had one thing in common: high intake of fatty fish. Fatty fish supplies a good deal of vitamin D, and without fatty fish (before the supplements and devices we have today), there was no way for northern people to have sufficient vitamin D. These people would eat fatty fish 2-3x/day. While we would not encourage that much fish, it is reasonable to say that we need to have some sort of plan for supporting vitamin D levels throughout winter, if direct sunlight is not sufficient.

Red Light Therapy. Also known as photobiomodulation, red light therapy stimulates mitochondrial activity, helps to balance our blue light exposure, can synthesize collagen in the skin, decreases inflammation, supports regulation of our circadian rhythm, and much more. It can also help mitigate the stress we feel from shorter days.

Sleeping St. Joseph

Sleep is a gift. It is a gift that offers rest, which was made sacred by our Lord on the seventh day of Creation. As discussed throughout these pages, sleep is an absolutely critical piece to achieving and maintaining good health. But it is also pleasant. Most people (when not in a state of stress) absolutely delight in sleep. It is a sweet reward following a day (hopefully) spent serving God, so often in small, mundane ways, yet nonetheless pleasing to Him. It is a much-needed bookend in our life, separating night from morning, allowing us to pause before rising again. The gift of sleep helps break up our to-do list, encouraging us to focus on today, for "sufficient for a day is its own evil" (Matthew 6:34).

If there was ever a saint who knew the value of a good sleep, it was our dear spiritual father, St. Joseph. It is quite obvious that he rested peacefully in the hands of the Father. In his *Consecration to St. Joseph*, Father Calloway writes, "[Joseph] liked to sleep. Sleep refreshed his soul. God communicated with St. Joseph when he slept, and he was a holier husband and father because of it." Pure of heart and faithful to God, Joseph embraced rest and became more receptive and responsive to God's will through it.

> "You are not wasting time when you rest. Sleep is pleasing to God.
> God will speak to you and refresh your soul when you sleep."
>
> — Father Calloway, *Consecration to Saint Joseph*

Father Mike Schmitz, in his *Bible in a Year* podcast, said early on that we were created for "leisure, labor, and love." Rest (and sleep) is a part of leisure — a gift that God wants us to take advantage of. He designed it such that it occupies a third of our life. What we read of St. Joseph in the Gospels demonstrates its importance. And yet, being far from God, or cut off through sin, can distort this gift to the point that it is anything but restful. A priest once joked to me, "Those who fall asleep easily have a light conscience." We know there are biological factors at play, for sure, that affect our falling and staying asleep, but there is wisdom in looking to the spiritual as well. Stress, anxiety, worries, a nagging conscience — these all weigh on the soul and frequently on the body. A big factor contributing to good health is safety — the body must feel safe, meaning it has enough of the right macronutrients, micronutrients, and calories without being overburdened by lifestyle factors or environment. Similarly, we must feel at peace in mind and heart. Burdened by our own sin, concerning ourselves with things outside of our control, dwelling on things we ought to hand to God — these lead to a heavy and weary spirit. And not the kind of weariness that leads to rest, but one that leads to consuming and fruitless thoughts, robbing us of grace.

Part of achieving better sleep, which pays dividends for our physical, mental, and spiritual health, is cultivating habits that bring our day to a peaceful end. Of course, any mortal sin should be confessed at the first chance so that we are not having to wrestle ourselves to sleep with that on our conscience. Otherwise, the Examen prayer is a great way to recollect our day with the Lord, noting where we felt His presence and where we didn't, where we responded to His grace and where we fell short. It is a time for gratitude and a time for contrition. Father Timothy Gallagher (author of *The Discernment of Spirits*, among many others) has a few beautiful episodes on the *Discerning Hearts* podcast where he explains the Examen prayer in depth and why it should be an integral part of our life.

Another practice that many find helpful is journaling. There are so many different approaches, and it really is about what works best for you. But if I may put forth a simple suggestion: Give it to Joseph. What do I mean by that? As we've discussed, there is an intimate relationship laid out in Scripture between God and Joseph through his sleep. From this comes a popular devotion to the "sleeping St. Joseph." Now, you could go out and get yourself a statue of sleeping St. Joseph, or you could just as well use an image. The idea is that we write out our intentions and lay them before Joseph,, asking his intercession. As "comfort of the afflicted," Joseph desires to offer us solace in our misery through his intercession. As "terror of demons," Joseph offers an example of quiet strength and trust in the Father in the face of the enemy's tricks and noise, attempting to steal our rest.

So if you find that you tend to have a lot weighing on your mind and heart as you turn in for the night, try writing out your greatest worries and burdens, turning them into intentions, and giving them to Joseph. As we all know, Joseph was given tremendous responsibility in caring for Mary and Jesus. Men of little faith would be utterly unequipped to fulfill this role, let alone have peace in the midst of it. Joseph demonstrates his complete trust in the Lord by the fact that he slept, and that he slept well. To rest peacefully amidst his circumstances, having full confidence in God's providence — this is trust.

So let us trust in Joseph's powerful intercession at the throne of God. And trust that Our Lord is responsive to Joseph, the foster father of Jesus, the spouse of the Mother of God, and the protector of His Church. When sleep seems like a battle, if we're allowing too much of the darkness of the world to cloud our minds and hearts — turn this all into prayer and entrust it to Joseph.

PART THREE

CONCLUSION

"All things have their season, and in their times all things pass under heaven. A time to be born and a time to die. A time to plant, and a time to pluck up that which is planted. A time to kill, and a time to heal. A time to destroy, and a time to build. A time to weep, and a time to laugh. A time to mourn, and a time to dance. A time to scatter stones, and a time to gather. A time to embrace, and a time to be far from embraces. A time to get, and a time to lose. A time to keep, and a time to cast away. A time to rend, and a time to sew. A time to keep silence, and a time to speak. A time of love, and a time of hatred. A time of war, and a time of peace."

— Ecclesiastes 3:1-8

The importance of seasons is evident in how they are built into almost every aspect of life. Spiritually speaking, we have the liturgical seasons given to us by the Church — times for fasting, times for feasting, special devotions marked at certain times of the year. When we look at creation, we see the earth move through her seasons without any prompting from us — each time of year part of a greater purpose in the service of sustaining life. Physiologically, we are creatures of seasons and rhythms. There are seasons of life — childhood, adolescence, young adulthood, parenting (and the many seasons within this calling), and so forth. There are more specific seasons for a woman as she moves through her reproductive years — pregnancy, postpartum, menopause. And there are the rhythms built into our biology — diurnal (night and day), circadian (24 hours), infradian (monthly, or female hormonal cycles).

To live ignorantly, or even obstinately opposed, to these ebbs and flows of life (so often done in the modern world) is to neglect our nature. And while it is crucial that we prioritize our spiritual health — finding our rhythm in the Church calendar — God desires that we also tend to our bodies, being restored through the many gifts He's placed within our grasp. Learning to integrate the two, with both the liturgical year given to us by the Church and creation given to us by the Creator Himself, is not about arduously seeking balance, but peacefully discovering harmony.

May this book, which was written to serve you in this pursuit, be a companion — for your journey towards wholeness — and a seed — for all the growth to come.

AMDG,
The Ember Team

"I want creation to penetrate you with so much admiration that everywhere, wherever you may be, the least plant may bring to you the clear remembrance of the Creator. If you see the grass of the fields, think of human nature, and remember the comparison of the wise Isaiah. 'All flesh is grass, and all the goodliness thereof is as the flower of the field.'"

— St. Basil the Great

Acknowledgments

This book has been a labor of love for years at this point, since it pulls from our whole archive of *The Ember Journal* to date. Many people have been a part of this journey, and it would simply not be possible without them all.

Katie's husband, Kevin, has done so much silent work for Ember over the years and has always encouraged her in this pursuit. Samantha's husband, Joseph, has spent many an evening caring for their children while she tended to her work on this apostolate. And to everyone else in our families who has helped us along the way — children, parents, siblings (also known as babysitters) — thank you!

So much of our content comes from women who have something meaningful to say — and a beautiful way of saying it. Our contributing writers have been so generous with their gifts, and to everyone who has allowed us to incorporate their work into this book, we are deeply grateful. A special thank you to Marisa, who has been our Ember chef all these years — your recipes are a delight and help to bring out our mission in a special way. Mackenzie, you have been a consistent rock for Ember all these years, never failing to offer the theology pieces that bring our *Journals* together. And Maria, your unique content on liturgical customs and traditions around the world has been an absolute gift to Ember (along with your editing!).

We are so grateful to the team at Sophia Institute for allowing us the opportunity to publish a book like this. We are so passionate about holistic wellness as it intersects with our Catholic faith, and it is such an honor to be able to publish this work through you.

Andrea and Alyse, your work with Ember is so valuable to us, and this book couldn't be a reality without your dedication and creativity!

Finally, we would be nowhere without our fantastic Ember community. There are many of you who have been around from the beginning, when Katie was meticulously overpacking each *Journal* in her living room. Your support and engagement are priceless, and this book is for you!

And to the Holy Spirit for always finding ways to spark creativity and carry everything through when we've felt empty or at a loss. Anything good of this work is completely of the Lord.

Deo gratias,
Katie, Samantha, and Elissa

THE EMBER JOURNAL CONTRIBUTORS

Courtney Cantu-Rice

Courtney Cantu-Rice is a wife, mother, and friend residing in small-town Texas. She is a registered nurse with a passion for writing. When she isn't chasing her beautiful toddler or writing, she loves to bake, go for long runs, or spend time with her Book Club friends over a delicious cup of coffee.

Lauren E. De Witt

Lauren is a Catholic convert, wife, and mother. After practicing law for seven years, Lauren "retired" to pursue a life dedicated to contemplative home-making: seeking union with God through continual prayer and wholehearted service to her family.

Virginia Elmer

Virginia is passionate about homeschooling, home-birthing, homesteading, and homemaking, with her four little children, her scientist/farmer husband, and their 60 (ish) farm animals.

Marisa Fredrickson

Residing in Nebraska with her husband and 5 children, Marisa enjoys cooking and creating beautiful seasonal food to share with loved ones.

Maria Fredriksson

Originally from the Midwest, Maria Fredriksson graduated from John Paul the Great Catholic University, worked on feature films in California, and started a theatre group in North Idaho before the lure of Shakespeare and political philosophy took her to the Wyoming School of Catholic Thought, where she met her husband at a literary music night. They enjoy immersing their family in integrated culture and fostering anything that's festive, formative, and home-crafted among the Wyoming Catholic College community and beyond. Her writing and editing have appeared in *The Ember Journal*, *European Conservative*, and various plays, and you can find her on Instagram at @mariameetsbeauty or https://delarose.shop where she focuses on bringing back traditional textile skills.

Eryn Goldstein

Eryn is a Catholic wife and mother and a Nutritious Movement certified Restorative Exercise Specialist. She loves to help people discover physical ease, strength, and joy through intentional movement.

Emily Hannon

Emily Hannon lives with her husband and five young children in her hometown of Pittsburgh, Pennsylvania. She is a lover of thrifting, growing flowers, and snapping photos of ordinary moments and miracles.

Megan Madden

Megan Madden is a wife to a theologian, mum of 6, and author of the books *Mary, Teach Me to be Your Daughter: Finding Yourself in the Blessed Mother* and *Through Storms and Still Waters: Finding Union with Christ in Suffering*, both with Ascension Press. You can find her on Instagram @amotherslace.

Emily Malloy

Emily Malloy is the food and floral design editor for TheologyofHome.com. Her book, *Theology of Home IV: Arranging the Seasons*, came out in fall 2023. She and her husband live in Mississippi with their four children.

Susanna Parent

Susanna Parent is a wife, mother, freelance writer, and speaker who lives in the Twin Cities with her husband and children. She is a graduate of Catholic Studies from the University of St. Thomas in St. Paul, Minnesota and, after working with the Archdiocese of St. Paul and Minneapolis, she now begins her mornings brewing French press coffee and snuggling up with her children on the couch to read (while trying not to spill her coffee). Her published work can be found at fiatandalily.blogpost.com.

Emily Patteson

Emily Patteson is a wife, mom, runner, sewist, chemist, and lover of Jesus. She enjoys writing about how the Lord works in everyday life and the connection between science and faith. Her best days include time spent with her family, at the beach, or in the adoration chapel.

Genie Shaw

Genie is a Catholic convert and second-generation homeschool mom to a passel of 9 bairns, deep in the heart of Texas where their little farmstead is modeled after the rhythm of monastic life and naturally observing the liturgical year. Genie writes the popular blog *Barefoot Abbey,* where cloister meets hearth, and is founder of the Feast Fast Feria Collective, a mentorship and community for busy Catholic mothers that takes the stress and guesswork out of liturgical living.

Theresa Thomas

Theresa lives in rural Missouri, is a wife to her husband Nick, and a mother to her three sons on earth and two children in Heaven. She and her husband have a strong devotion to the Holy Family, and she is passionate about homemaking and living out the vocation of wife and mother. You will most often find her chasing her toddler and chickens around her yard with an ice coffee in hand, milking their family cow, tending to her garden, picking wildflowers, or praying her daily Rosary while washing dishes, folding laundry, or making dinner.

Anna Truxillo

Anna lives in South Louisiana with her husband and two little boys. As a holistic health practitioner, she trusts in the wisdom of God's design of the body and seeks to help other mothers come to know and honor that design through functional movement and nourishment, so they may better live out their vocation of motherhood. At home with her boys and coffee in hand, she strives to cultivate a Christ-centered and nourishing home.

Mackenzie Worthing

Mackenzie Worthing is a wife and mother who lives in Omaha, Nebraska. Once she was a student studying English and Theology at the University of St. Thomas and the Augustine Institute. She now uses her degrees to write and edit very part time when she isn't baking bread or dancing with her children.

Bibliography

Introduction
- Bhardwaj, Raju Lal, et al. "An Alarming Decline in the Nutritional Quality of Foods: The Biggest Challenge for Future Generations' Health." *Foods*, vol. 13, no. 6, 1 Jan. 2024, p. 877, www.mdpi.com/2304-8158/13/6/877, https://doi.org/10.3390/foods13060877.

Foundations
- Price, Weston A, and Trung Nguyen. "Nutrition and Physical Degeneration: A Comparison of Primitive and Modern Diets and Their Effects," EnCognitive.com, 8 Jan. 2016.

- Lane, Melissa M., et al. "Ultra-Processed Food Exposure and Adverse Health Outcomes: Umbrella Review of Epidemiological Meta-Analyses." *BMJ*, vol. 384, no. 8419, 28 Feb. 2024, p. e077310, www.bmj.com/content/384/bmj-2023-077310, https://doi.org/10.1136/bmj-2023-077310.

- Walker, Matthew P. *Why We Sleep: Unlocking the Power of Sleep and Dreams*. New York, Scribner, An Imprint Of Simon & Schuster, Inc, 28 Sept. 2017.

- Pizzorno, Joseph E. *The Toxin Solution : How Hidden Poisons in the Air, Water, Food, and Products We Use Are Destroying Our Health--and What We Can Do to Fix It*. New York, Harperone, 2018.

- Environmental Working Group. "Body Burden: The Pollution in Newborns." EWG, 14 July 2005, www.ewg.org/research/body-burden-pollution-newborns.

- Bowman, Katy. *Move Your DNA*. Sequim, Washington, Propriometrics Press, 2017.

Through the Seasons
- Nestor, James. Breath: *The New Science of a Lost Art*. New York, Riverhead Books, 2020.

- Brewer, Thomas H. *Metabolic Toxemia of Late Pregnancy*. Aahcc, 2004.

- Carmen Acevedo Butcher, and Saint Hildegard. *St. Hildegard of Bingen, Doctor of the Church: A Spiritual Reader*. Brewster, Mass., Paraclete Press, 2013.

Katie Gearns

Katie Gearns is a wife, homeschooling mother, and Nutritional Therapy Practitioner living in St. Paul, Minnesota. Her great loves are the richness of the Catholic faith, family culture, parish community, and all things wellness.

Samantha Worthing

Samantha Worthing is a wife and mother of three, Nutritional Therapy Practitioner, photographer, and avid gardener. She lives in Omaha, Nebraska, where she spends her time homeschooling, cooking with her family, and growing lots of flowers.

Elissa Voss

Elissa Voss is the Ember photographer and recently moved from San Diego, California to St. Paul, Minnesota. She finds joy in embracing Catholic traditions and discovering a good antique shop. Her desire is to create a beautiful space, prepare a nourishing meal, and pursue a simpler life.

Sophia Institute

Sophia Institute is a nonprofit institution that seeks to nurture the spiritual, moral, and cultural life of souls and to spread the gospel of Christ in conformity with the authentic teachings of the Roman Catholic Church.

Sophia Institute Press fulfills this mission by offering translations, reprints, and new publications that afford readers a rich source of the enduring wisdom of mankind.

Sophia Institute also operates the popular online resource CatholicExchange.com. *Catholic Exchange* provides world news from a Catholic perspective as well as daily devotionals and articles that will help readers to grow in holiness and live a life consistent with the teachings of the Church.

In 2013, Sophia Institute launched Sophia Institute for Teachers to renew and rebuild Catholic culture through service to Catholic education. With the goal of nurturing the spiritual, moral, and cultural life of souls, and an abiding respect for the role and work of teachers, we strive to provide materials and programs that are at once enlightening to the mind and ennobling to the heart; faithful and complete, as well as useful and practical.

Sophia Institute gratefully recognizes the Solidarity Association for preserving and encouraging the growth of our apostolate over the course of many years. Without their generous and timely support, this book would not be in your hands.

www.SophiaInstitute.com
www.CatholicExchange.com
www.SophiaTeachers.org

Sophia Institute Press is a registered trademark of Sophia Institute.
Sophia Institute is a tax-exempt institution as defined by the
Internal Revenue Code, Section 501(c)(3). Tax ID 22-2548708.